Hanging On For Dear Life

To order additional copies, please contact us.
BookSurge, LLC
www.booksurge.com
1-866-308-6235
orders@booksurge.com

GARY
WEIBYE

HANGING ON
FOR DEAR LIFE

Gary O. Weibye

2004

Hanging On For Dear Life

TABLE OF CONTENTS

Acknowledgements: Thanks to Vicky Lee for the cover photo, Scott Baldassari for the interior scenic art and cartoons, Beverly Knight for being "Wifey" and critic, and Jasper, Arkansas, for being itself.

INTRODUCTION

There are no bars in Jasper, Arkansas, so the way this goes is, a guy walks into the Chamber of Commerce information center, and he says to the lady, "Nice little town."

She says, "Yep. Like no other town anywhere."

"That's the way I hear it," he says, a little edge to his voice.

"Gee, what have you heard?" she asks him.

"Well, I'm into real estate, and I've talked to a few folks locally. So, naturally, I have questions."

"Sure you have. Want a nice cup of coffee?" she says. "Today's brew is called Bifferdoodle."

"No, thank you."

"Are you sure? You're an hour and a half from the nearest Starbuck's."

"No, I'm fine."

"Okay, shoot—questions," she says, having some coffee herself.

"Well, availability of resources is up front here," he says, looking at a notebook. "This is canoe country, so where do I rent a canoe?"

"At a motel, half a block from here. That's the closest."

"And if I want...say...fried chicken?"

"The gas station is fastest."

"And I hear I can get gasoline at the super market."

"Well, yes. Spaying and neutering at the high school twice a year, horticultural advice at the old nursing home...It's a small town."

"And is it true that if you want sand & gravel around here you go to the judge?"

"Well, yes...that *is* how it is done."

"And if you want justice, you go to the doctor?"

"Well, that's his name—Justice. Dr. Justice. Never thought about that."

"Uh huh. And if you want chain saws, batteries, or tires, you go to ...?"

"The feed store."

"Ah. And if you want art or pizza, you go to the...uh...bakery?"

"Yes. The bakery."

"But donuts are completely out of the question, I understand."

"Well, not always. You can get chicken at the Pizza Pro, too—and you can get pizza at the gas station, now that I think about it. Are you in the market for some nice fresh spices?" she asks, nodding at the merchandise in the store.

"No, thank you."

"Hand-made greeting cards? Hand-woven place mats?"

"I don't think so. Now, if I want opera locally, I go to The Mercantile, is that right?"

"On Saturday night. Comedy, too—Broadway, rock, even gospel. We really get it goin' over at The Mercantile. And even the sad songs make us feel better."

"I understand that the folks in the kitchen at the cafe over there can sing everything from light opera to rock & roll."

"Yeah. And there's a talented sculptor who is the best keyboard man around, and a social worker who writes and performs her own songs."

"Lotta multi-tasking," he mumbles, taking notes.

"Yeah. There are road workers, foresters, electrical workers, and bulldozer guys around here who play stringed instruments. One construction guy plays a saw! Girl over at the Junk Museum is a singer. I guess we are a quirky bunch, come to think about it."

"I guess so. What do I do if I want to see a movie?" says the guy, fiddling with his pen.

"The library or the grocery store can fix you right up. Or you can go to Harrison. Wanna buy a photo? a sun catcher? a mobile?" she says, waving at the goods around her.

"I haven't the time."

"How about a clock!"

"Not just yet. Now, let me see: your city dump has a million-dollar view, I understand, and its chief function is salvage? And junk is for sale everywhere?"

"Well, one man's trash..."

"Is another man's treasure. Right. And, you can get a brake job here, if only your brakes hold long enough to get you down the hill, around the hairpin curves, and into the town?"

"Guess so. Gotta gear down, slow down, and stay on top of those brakes."

"But at the bottom of the hill. And the town is the Elk Capital, you say?"

"Yes. It's on our logo..."

"On the Little Buffalo River—with the Big Buffalo River nearby?" He checks his notes.

"I guess you could say that. Elk Capital—Buffalo River. That's us. We have lots of brochures here..."

"And you can get Buffalo Wings at the cafe, but no Elk Wings?"

"Don't be ridiculous. Elks don't have wings."

"Uh huh. I guess you're right," the guy says, backing off a little.

"Those buffalo wings are actually from chickens, of course," she says. "We raise a lot of chickens around here. We wake up to roosters crowing."

"Of course you do. And you have *Guinea Crossing* signs in your town, but no traffic lights?"

"Yeah. Guineas. It's true. They render a service—bug control. We protect those guineas. You don't see that a lot, I suppose."

"You suppose right. And wild turkeys run around in people's yards here?"

"That's the way we like it. Eagles overhead, hunting—buzzards too, waiting. Great little town."

"Ah ha..." the guy says with grave and artificial dignity. "A bird problem." He strokes his chin pensively.

"And half the trucks that come through here are full of chicken waste. I see what you're getting at," says the lady.

"Ah, the trucks. This seems like the last place in the world you would want to bring an 18-Wheeler, right?—and yet you see them all too often."

"One of our chief local industries is winching those suckers out of the ditches and setting them back on their wheels—or peeling them off rock walls. But we are here for our clientele. And if you really have to have a traffic light, Sir, they've got them in Harrison. Boone County. Need a map? I've got maps!"

"No, thank you." He mumbles, consults his list. "I hear you have an inventor out here close by."

"Yeah. He puts a container of stuff in a microwave oven, heats it up, and it comes out ice cream. Typical, I guess."

"Yes, I suppose that would happen here. And they say the place is 'churchy.' I've heard that the language over at the pool hall is antiseptic: no cussing, no bad language—no drinking, no smoking."

"That's at the Senior Center. Respectful, country folks. Sweet people—Salt of the Earth. True enough. Polite language. Wanna buy a book? We've got writers...local poets..."

"Maybe later. I've also heard that the only place Hell is mentioned locally is in church. Is that right?"

"I wouldn't know. But out here it's easy to forget about Hell. Oh, and write this down: we nationalized the Buffalo River to prevent a dam! They were going to build a dam. We didn't want to have a dam because we are peculiar and don't even want to see a dam or say dam or think about a dam," she says, giggling a little. "How's that!" (See, she's getting a little testy with the guy now.)

"No lottery?"

"Not a chance. I guess we're just lucky."

"And you can't get a drink here?" he grins suspiciously.

"Do you want to drink and then drive our roads?"

"Not me. I've also heard that when you're out here in some God-forsaken, hellish, rocky wasteland, you call that Paradise!"

"Yep. Very beautiful. But we don't believe anything is God-forsaken. Be careful."

"Sorry," he said quietly. "It *is* gorgeous around here, if you dare to look."

"Gotta be careful., though. Gotta park your car, set the brake, and *then* look. Have you checked out all of our paintings?"

"They're very nice."

"All local artists. Make you a deal!"

"Not now, Dear. I understand that the area is a mecca for 4-wheelers, dirt bikes, and motorcycles—but you can't get one repaired here?"

"Well, there's no special shop for that. We make canoes here—for the river. Lots of floaters. A canoe we can fix."

"You've got a strange little place going here, you know that?"

"One of a kind."

"Most of the hillbillies, I hear, are new people?" The guy has some kind of print-out he keeps looking at now.

"Not the real ones. The new people admire the hillbillies and envy their values and skills—try to be like them. And, by the way, a hillbilly? He'll fix that 4-wheeler for you in a New York minute."

"Right. And I understand that the woodcutters take care of the forests around here, too—is that right?"

"Yep—like the farmers take care of the crops. And if you see someone out here on the streets operating heavy equipment, that could be the mayor!"

"A likely story. Oh, and about the police: where is the local speed trap?" Now he's overtly taking notes.

"Well, we have First Responders for that. Around here, speed IS the trap. Gotta gear down, slow down. If you speed, we have folks who will get you down out of the trees, pull you up out of the canyons, or sponge you off the stone walls. EMTs, High Angle Rescue teams. Gotcha covered."

"What do you do if you want to dance?"

"Friday night, City Hall, in the kitchen. Live band and sandwiches."

"What do you people do for exercise?"

"We hike, we ride, we swim, we garden, we climb mountains, we canoe, we rescue tourists, and we work—and that's just the older people. The young are the really active ones."

"And everybody is a crafter, it seems," he says, looking around the store.

"Nobody is just one thing. Everybody has to create. Around here, they just do it! Have you seen the T-shirts, the pot holders, the woodwork, scroll saw work? Cut you a deal! We have jewelry. How about a bird's nest!"

"Perhaps another time. What if I need something vital—like a pair of glasses?"

"Then you have to be able to see well enough to drive some of the most challenging roads in North America and get yourself to Wal-Mart. Or a neighbor could take you. What's your point?"

"Well, it's hard to get out of here."

"Hard to get here, too—takes a lot of luck and clean living to get here."

"Interesting. Uh...what is that beautiful new building out there along Seven North?"

"Nursing home, our newest building."

"The newest building is for the oldest people?"

"Sure. An investment. They deserve it. And the *busiest* building, other than the schools, is the Senior Center, for the *retired* folks—right there on the main drag. Can't miss it. Way we figure it, it's in everybody's future and in everybody's interest."

"What about technology? Are you up to date? Got all the new toys? What about cell phones, for example?"

"No problem," says the lady. "Just take your phone and climb Round Top Mountain—you can talk to Guam from up there. Say, how about a pair of sequined blue jeans!"

"Sequined blue jeans? You've got sequined blue jeans? I have searched everywhere for those things—uh...to give as gifts, of course."

"Of course. We'll fix you right up. Stand by."

***

Well, you get the picture. Sooner or later, the place gets you. Out of all the world, this is where we have chosen to spend our retirement years, our "golden" years, our remaining years. The town is down mountain from where we live, and it is our lifeline and probably our destination when we are through clinging to the ridge "up top." Wifey and I—refugees from city lives and careers—are trying to fit in, fall into stride, match the pace, and perhaps belong. We are a little zany ourselves. We are here with our new friends, fighting Time and Fortune and Gravity, and we are hanging on for dear life.

The stories and sketches presented here are about people *like* those we know and places and activities *like* those we have encountered. Most of the names have been changed, and the personalities have been scrambled, shuffled, and muddled—for the sake of clarity. Time has been "fooled around with," too. Mountains have been moved, and the weather fixed. All of this has been done by someone who loves the place and "wouldn't change a thing." Go figure. Still, the Truth is in there somewhere—almost everywhere. That's how fiction works sometimes.

Gary Weibye

SHARING THE WONDER

Those first few sunrises bursting over our breakfast table and flooding our rooms with new light sent us scurrying about the move-in debris of our unsatisfactory house groping for cameras and sketch pads, pens and brushes, anything to get it down on paper, somehow, and pass it all on to the poor devils who missed it.

And we had to do it with our free eye, you see—keeping our gaze fixed upon a rolling pink cloudbank about to yield dragons or sailing ships, and feeling around for the video camera with one hand while somehow holding onto the view with the other, not to let the beauty get away.

"My God! Look at that!" I would gasp as a geyser of heaven-hued vapor would leap out of a fold in the valley floor two miles away and then join other rioting clouds below—off to the East there, under Red Rock.

"I saw," Wifey would say, and then we would want everyone to see. I wanted to snap the definitive photo, draw or paint or tell the story of the sunrise and the mists of morning in my valley like it had never been done before. But I had no drawing or painting genes, and a thousand photos wouldn't get it.

"Good Lord," I would mumble, panning the vista. "Just look at that! So...beautiful." And then I would lower the camera, and stand mute, and just let it in. Beautiful. What a pathetic word.

Eventually, I saw the humor in the situation. It was melodrama! I realized that every morning of my life from this point on, as long as I had senses, I could receive the morning and be truly overwhelmed in every cell of my being, and never get it all. I could click still pictures and sweep the whole panorama—store film and tape and whatever—and babble platitudes fading away to gibberish—and never get it down, never pass it on, never save the sunrise for the next witness. And that was the joke.

"Hum-drum," in this new existence of ours, meant spectacular, commonplace grandeur, on the way to Wal-Mart, breathtaking vistas, beside the road on the way to the post office—transfixed tourists, blocking traffic on the way to Bob's Grocery—astounding, photographable wonders, intercepting us on our way to Bingo. Our county dump indeed had a million dollar view. I was amazed. I drove through a rainbow one day bringing a load of chicken manure up the mountain for our garden. Just mowing the grass, I could get lost in the spectacle, lose my place, drift off, and just sit down and smile. Sometimes I would forget to eat. I tried poetry (everybody does), and I fell in, well past the words, and ended up silent and stunned. It was extreme! I felt a need for perspective.

***

Then one morning I was driving into town after some groceries and some nails, and I saw Double-Dog Darrell's horse at Scenic Point. I had to stop for that. Certainly he could give me perspective—help me adjust and sort it all out. In this new phase of my life, he was my mentor, my seer, my guru. I thought more of him than he thought of me, but I needed his input. As he once said, "I am a barometer; you are a dipstick."

It was easy to locate Darrell that day because a puddle of tourists had developed at the base of the wooden tower someone built there so that, after reaching the highest point around, people could climb up a little higher. (That's all I know. Boggles the mind.)

Anyway, they were looking up, and Double-Dog was at the top of the tower with all four of his wolves, and his crow was sitting on his shoulder, and he had the patch over his eye that day, and he was looking enigmatic as hell, eye fixed on the horizon in Missouri to the North. He was portraying the rustic "philosopher of yarn and saga" that he had carefully invented for the tourists—and me, I guess. The tourists were silent, and they were gazing at Double-

Dog rather than The View. He had their attention. Go figure. But that was what Double-Dog Darrell was about. He had become mystical. He had crossed over from Man to Myth, and he belonged to everyone now.

"I'll handle this," I said as I stepped through the knot of people (inbound from everywhere, I suppose). I climbed the wooden steps as they gazed at me. I couldn't help noticing that bib overalls are just made for climbing steps. They do not bind or fetter. Others had tried the steps, of course, but the wolves had discouraged them. But these wolves had known me for months. I wasn't sure about Double-Dog. Sometimes he pretended not to know me at all.

At the top, I was respectfully silent for a minute or two, and I scanned the scene. Breathtaking, as usual. (So were the steps.) The Inscrutable One was not talking. He was booted and caped, and he was "meditating." Time passed.

"I don't want to become inured to the dazzle," I finally told Double-Dog. "I don't want ever to get my fill, become sated with it." That's the way I started the conversation.

"You won't become immune. You won't grow callous. Every day, it'll just knock your socks off! But then, you'll go barefooted." Darrell knew my passion for metaphor, and fed me.

"Whaat?"

"You won't reach the point where you're unmoved. You will be moved. But you will function anyway." Double-Dog had lived in the mystic places in the county—high and low—in vales and glens, on mountaintops and in caves, outdoors and inside, in all seasons. And he had thought about things. "Evidently, since you get it, and since you live it every day, it is yours, and you deserve it. You have been given Wonder. Drink it in, and then get your butt down to the hardware store and quit feelin' so much." He could not spend pity on someone over-awed with beauty.

"Just get over it, huh?"

"No. You never get over it. You absorb it with gratitude, and you go on about your affairs." He stopped talking and re-positioned me so that the tourists could see *him* better. In the process, he switched his patch to the other eye. He gestured in an exaggerated fashion, pointing at something far away. This was a performance, and I was part of it now.

"Shocks, traumas, horribly ugly things are like that, too. Death is like that. You pause, you don't stop. You have to keep movin'—keep the wind beneath your wings, or you'll drop. Some are better equipped to receive all this than others, and some are better at movin' on. *You* have to toughen up. *You* live here now. *You* stayed. Enjoy. Your capacity will increase. You will develop *capacity*."

"I can take in more?"

"You will learn. Look at these pathetic creatures," he said, gesturing at the tourists below—who, I am sure, thought I was up there preventing a suicide. "They have no capacity. Even they could grow. But they would have to get off the road and stay." Then he shifted his gaze. "Go to town and get your nails."

"How did you know I needed nails?"

"I have intuitions not understood by normal men," said Double-Dog Darrell. "I have awareness developed and honed and perfected..."

"Bull roar," I countered.

"Yeah, well there's a note stickin' up out of the bib in your overalls," he said, peeking out from under the eye patch. "Better get that milk, too. God knows you don't want to get that wife of yours upset. Now go. My public awaits." He gave the crowd a profile—his best one. I left him there, thinking deep thoughts, posing for the tourists.

When one of the curious travelers stopped me at the bottom of the steps and cautiously asked me what was going on at the top of the tower, I said, "A man is thinking."

Another stopped me and asked, "Are you the sheriff, Sir?"

"No," I said quietly, "I am just a humble carpenter."

And I walked away as mysteriously as I had approached, I hope. I don't know how that looks with the bib overalls. But you have to get the ridiculous with the sublime sometimes. I love it when that happens, and I would want it that way if I were a tourist. Tourists have expectations.

***

Okay, it is ridiculous, but I get to believing everything, even when we are just baiting the tourists. Double-Dog Darrell and I allowed ourselves to wax philosophical up there; but, after all, we were at Scenic Point, and it was morning, and at our feet lay the valley and the fifty-mile view, and we saw an eagle from above—dark, over a carpet of milky fog, and he was hunting. And we saw, we saw! We had a right to some philosophy.

But I picked up the key word, too: gratitude. "Absorb it with gratitude." I moved on, hoping that my gratitude was obvious. I was grateful for every aspect of my new life in the mountains. I gripped the wheel of my modest little truck heading downhill, screaming through the hairpin curves, and mumbling joyful Thank You's—for good measure. Around our mountain, folks believe those mumblings are heard.

CARGO KELLY IS AMONG US!

I recognized "Cargo Kelly" the minute I saw him, because I had lived in the city where he was notorious. I knew that he had created a veritable imports empire by promising same-day delivery—"We'll have you tucked in by ten tonight"—and I could not imagine what he was doing out along Scenic Byway Seven—right in my driveway.

It was a cool morning, and I was at the mail box just across the highway, and I was dressed in jeans and a long-sleeved sweatshirt—nothing remarkable. I say that because hundreds of times I had seen Cargo Kelly wearing a wicker cabinet, right on my TV, back in the city.

His nauseating, incessant, day and night commercials were a part of life in most households. He had this wicker-looking box with holes cut in it for his face, arms, and legs, and every time you turned on the TV to catch a show or some news, there he was, screaming his hype with his high, untrained voice, jumping up and down with a fist full of dollars, goading and nagging and interfering, just a half a beat out of sync. I had experienced nightmares about a truckload of peacock feathers or scented bamboo lamp shades being dumped on our doorstep in the city—just before ten p.m., of course—by this same Cargo Kelly, in person, all dolled up in his wicker cabinet outfit.

I remembered him, all too well, and I remembered inquiring into putting together a group of investors to pay him to get off the air. He was that bad—a real "obnoxioso." Of course, it would never have worked: he was making a mint and he couldn't be bought. And there was no "Anti-Cargo Kelly" chip available back then, so he was there all the time. Nothing could be done.

But here he was in my driveway. And, yes, I had time to think all those thoughts as I walked across the highway toward his car: a sudden, devastating mind storm! I went into denial, too, but there it was: a Lexus, I noticed, with Texas plates. The guy had a pinkish sweater tied around his neck. (I could never get away with that.) It was him, all right. A handsome, smooth-looking, very put-together lady was with him, sitting in the right hand seat—no longer a "girl," but well-maintained. No wicker outfit was anywhere in sight.

"Howdy," I said, approaching the car. "Can I help you?"

He jumped right out of the car and grabbed my hand and shook it. "Hi, I am Morty Kretzler. I just absolutely by-god cannot believe what I've been seeing up here. I've been up and down this stretch of road for half an hour, and I can't decide what's the prettiest view. Looks like you've decided." Pleats and creases in the pants, one-owner shoes, probably. Impressive.

"Yeah, Wifey and I live here now. We like *our* view." I tried to give a firm handshake, but he had my hand the way a politician gets your hand—all the gripping was him.

"Retired here, huh?" He tried to look past the house and into The View out back. Everybody does that. I ignored it at first because I wanted him to wait, maybe a long time.

"Yeah. We dropped out, moved out, kicked back, and here we are."

"That's what I'm gonna do," Cargo Kelly said. "Gonna buy me a mountain and build a big old log cabin. Then I'm gonna just gradually move out here and live like a human being."

I couldn't believe I had him right there in my driveway. He had spoiled my dinner many a time with his commercials. Here was the voice, the hyperkinetic bounding about, the whole routine. It was definitely The Annoying Cargo Kelly of nightmare and legend. I tried to alibi for him and entertain the thought that the man had to make a living, after all. He made me sick, but he was a celebrity. I was in the presence of fame, or infamy. And who was I, right? I was just mildly impressed—wowed a little. No time for snobbery. I just had this nagging history of hating him.

"You're going to retire? Well, you couldn't find a better place," I said honestly. "Wifey and I have never regretted a minute of it."

"Wifey. I like that. So, you just quit the rat race and blew outa town. That's what I'm gonna do: get myself out here away from it all."

Then he changed gears completely and said to me, "Do I look familiar to you at all?"

"Familiar enough for all practical purposes," I said, trying not to be obviously evasive.

"We'll have you tucked in by ten tonight!" he offered, as a broad hint, I suppose.

"Huh?"

"I sell imports, you know." I saw suspicion, but hope, too, in his face.

"Imports?" I asked innocently. (It would spoil things if this guy knew that I knew him. We had absolutely nothing in common, and I didn't think this was ever going to bloom into a friendship, but I wanted to avoid the awkwardness of the twilight zone between Have's and Have Not's. As long as it was just man-to-man, we could talk.)

"Yeah. Reeds, Romance, and Rattan! Beads, bamboo, and brass!"

"Oh."

"I'm Cargo Kelly," he said significantly. "I deliver—sometimes in person."

"Well, Mr. Kelly…uh…Cargo…hello. Welcome to the hills." (I know I was taking some license, but I did welcome him—not on behalf of the hills or my neighbors or the town, but I did extend a welcome. I am a sensitive, polite person. All of us in our family were always very tender hearted. Still, if anything goes wrong, this guy is not my fault. I insist.)

I tried to sort of gaze off into the view, but he got in close, right between me and anything else I wanted to look at.

"I dress up like a wicker cabinet, you know—on TV—and I come on fifteen or twenty times a night and harass people about

Indonesian trundle beds and Chinese incense and cane coffee tables..."

"You dress up like a wicker cabinet?" (I used a very quizzical mug here. Disbelief.)

"Yeah, and I wave my arms and yell about teakwood jungle battle masks and South American and African wall hangings and Filipino arctic wear."

"And how does that make you feel?" (I thought I'd give him a shot of Dr. Phil, just for the fun of it.)

"Well, I used to feel pretty good about it, because I made a ton of money in that outfit. But lately, I've had my regrets." He paused and studied me. "You sure you don't know me?"

And then I saw something that just won me over and turned me around: Cargo Kelly was getting old! And he was carrying a load of doubt! His hair was a bit too dark, I could tell. Someone had done things to his face, too, but he was aging anyway. In the sunlight, all was evident. And I could see that, like me, he had thought somehow he might turn out to be immune to all that.

"I want to get out of the city before I lose much more time, and I want to be where there are real people." He was craning again, and maneuvering for a look at our View.

"Well, I haven't seen anybody around here wearing a wicker cabinet, but you might be able to fit in. Better not buy a whole mountain, though—unless you intend to preserve it for posterity." Then I thought, what the hey! "Come on out back and I'll show you something."

So I took Morty Kretzler, alias Cargo Kelly, out back, through the little wind tunnel between the house and the garage to where he could see what Wifey and I see every day. The lady in the car did not wish to move, and appeared to be heavily into a magazine. I asked, and she was theoretically Mrs. Kretzler. He was not excited about that. It was one of those old tired marriages, and his journey was her journey. I started liking him.

Morty walked out back with me—two arms and two legs, a mortal man after all—and fell into The View, just like anybody else. "You live like this every day, all year long?"

"Yeah. Hate the house—love the view."

"Yeah," he said, looking at our humble abode, "I guess so. I could put you into some nice Danish Modern plastic cane lawn furniture—or some real wicker stuff, but…"

"No thank you. We've already got one of your wicker chairs."

Well, I blew that, right there. I just blurted that out like I had no brains at all. And he snapped to it immediately, and I was trapped. I wanted to edit the thing and say "those wicker chairs" or "a wicker chair," but the damage was done. My game was over.

"You've got one of MY chairs? Where are you from?"

"Houston," I confessed, trying to be casual.

"Then you do know me. I was right."

"Yeah. I just didn't want to know you that way."

"What's that supposed to mean?"

"Well, I lived there a long time, and so did you. I remember when you had a Grand Opening Sale that lasted two years, and then you had a Going Out of Business Sale for four years! You had truckload sales and boxcar sales, and contingency sales—I got sick of your sales!"

"And *me*!"

"Oh, yeah. You had an Early Retirement Sale ten years ago and three years of a Lost Our Lease sale that I know about. I hated you."

"How 'bout all those Spring Sales, January White Sales, Inventory Adjustment Blow-outs, and Back-to-School Bashes!"

"You even did a Mother-in-Law Went Home Sale."

"And a Hernia Sale. And it was real—the hernia, anyway."

"Made me tired, if I can be perfectly honest. 'We'll have you tucked in by ten tonight.' Aaaarrrrggh!" I actually tried to do his voice.

"Hey, it's not easy to convince people that bean bag chairs are important in winter—or that everybody needs the coziness of cane coffee table, some rice mats and chopsticks, and bamboo room screens. I'm good at this stuff."

"You wanna know the truth? The real truth?"

"Sure. I'm rich. Hell, tell me the truth."

"Well, Cargo, uh...Morty... the technique didn't work on me! Every night at dinner time, that high tinny voice, that ridiculous costume, the mistimed gestures and jumps, the annoying slogans—you and that tribe of used car salesmen!—made me angry! And during the news at ten: Good Grief!"

"But you watched."

"You were there everywhere all the time!"

"You bought a chair from me."

"Yeah."

He had me. I knew that he wanted to win everybody—not just a majority, everybody. Back in the classroom, I wanted every kid—every one of them—in the palm of my hand. Nothing less would be acceptable. I knew this guy. We finally had something in common.

"About five million people in Houston/Galveston area—maybe more with Huntsville, Livingston, Conroe, La Port, Texas City. If just a small percentage of those people pick up a wicker chair now and then..."

"That's a lot of wicker."

"A *lot* of wicker—and peacock feathers and candles and pottery."

"Tell me: is it true that there is a school for characters like Cargo Kelly and the foaming-at-the-mouth used car salesman and the squeaky carpet guy that will do a room for $59?—a school about how to do those annoying commercials?"

"Sure. I'm heavily invested in one. People have to be screamed at a lot to get new car fever. Worse with imports. But I'm gonna get out of all that—all of it. We're gonna have a legit liquidation sale, I'm gonna burn my wicker cabinet outfit right on TV, and I'm gonna pull out. Well, I might bronze the outfit."

"What brought this on?" He looked to me like he could go on for years.

"Prostate. Up in the night all the time, peeing. Stomach crap. Gray hair. Wrinkles. Started hearing the clock ticking, looking into the mirror, slowing down. That was two years ago. I've been running around trying to decide whether I can cut retirement or not. And I have to find a place where people can forgive and forget."

"Forgive you!"

"Yeah—for making them sick all those years!"

Well, we had a little laugh about that, and I tried to be honest with him about our neighbors—many of whom had some Houston roots. It would have to be a complete transition—perhaps a slow one. He could be easily recognized. I could imagine a cadre of ex-Houston consumers descending upon the retired Cargo Kelly with rolls of duct tape to silence him permanently. Or peasants with pitchforks. *As I warned him, you don't know who is living out here in these hills.*

We joked about how he would have to grow a beard, maybe have a little plastic surgery, stay off TV, and never EVER wear a wicker cabinet again. He would have to maintain a low profile, not flaunt his money, maybe get a gray pony tail going—and a distinctive hat with the all-important personalized hatband—and a pair of overalls for social occasions. He would need some quilted plaid shirts made in Bangladesh, some rugged boots, maybe a full set of quilted brown coveralls for winter. Lots of camouflage accessories. He'd need 4-wheel drive, maybe an ATV, and a generator of some kind. Maybe a tattoo.

I offered to help him with a complete make-over. I told him about the local feed store—Manhood, Wardrobe, and Tool headquarters locally. But we were in separate classes, socially, and I had few illusions: we were never going to be buddies. My help I would freely give, but that would obligate him too much, and he would never be able to live with that. I understood. He would have to just buy that expertise from someone he could throw away. We had quite a talk, though, and I promised that I would not mention his plans to anybody. He left me, saying, "See you around the mountains."

***

Wifey was intrigued when I told her about the visit. I tried to sound unimpressed, but Wifey knew. I was running around there star-struck—like a babbling child. But I got over that soon and chalked it up to Life in the Mountains. (Heck, Andy Williams could drive up any minute—or Shoji Tabushi! Maybe even the Incredible Acrobats of China! Branson is just up the road.)

The whole thing was spoiled when I tried to use the wicker chair that we had around but seldom used. It got hold of the sweater her mother knitted for me, and I made the whole house look like a game of Cat's Cradle before I snapped to what was going on. I say it raveled; most folks say it unraveled. Both are accepted. Wifey donated the chair to the Humane Society Thrift Shop, and it was gone.

***

The remarkable thing is, he did it. "There are a lot of new people around," I heard someone say down in the village. "There are places being built, there is land being bought. Never seen so many log cabins..." You can't get away with much, really. People pay attention, and they are smart. And out there, high up on an "undisclosed" mountain, there is a very large log cabin owned by a mysterious city guy who spends a little more time there each month, but is seldom seen. People see a lot of helicopter activity around there, sometimes at night, and nobody gets close, even at night.

And one Saturday night I saw Morty Kretzler/Cargo Kelly with a handsome, smooth lady—down at The Mercantile in the village—letting in some local music. I insist. A very imaginative disguise, but it's him—more Morty than Cargo now, but it's him. We exchanged nods. Looks to me like he's going for the pony tail thing. He's trying to blend in.

But that wicker cabinet at Emma's Museum of Junk? That's not him.

INCIDENT AT THE LOW-WATER BRIDGE

Moose Vandergrift's tragedy is that his name is neither a nickname nor a misnomer. Apparently, about fifty-odd years ago, his parents looked into the puddle of swaddling clothes and said, "Let's name it Moose." So, I suppose it is there on his birth certificate, his service papers, his driver's license, his GED, his passport, and now his AARP card. His folks gave fair warning to the world.

Moose has good intentions. He wants nothing more than to be a part of the many worthy community efforts of the county, especially when heavy work is involved. His idea is that when brute force is needed, he is the man for the job, and he does not like to be left out. I learned that early, and Moose became my friend, and he protects me now. Just a word to the wise. Moose Vandergrift has my back.

There is a story that, late one cloudy afternoon, Moose happened upon a stricken vehicle along one of the really remote back roads, at a low-water bridge (a "ford" in the river), and stopped to render aid. In the mountains, such places are not rare: when the water is low, you can drive across the riverbed; when the water is high, you don't attempt it unless you can put up with a great deal of humiliation and terror and wetness. Upon this occasion, though, the water was low, and the vacationer simply "dropped a tranny" right there in the middle of the river, and came to an abrupt halt. That was the story, anyway.

Moose happened upon the scene innocently enough. He routinely prowls the back roads of the county. You could encounter him anywhere. Moose has a "disability" designation and receives a government check—and he is basically idle, bored. I could never decide what his disability was, and I had too much class to ask. (Well, I was afraid to ask.) I heard someone say that Moose is "not right." Maybe it is his little speech problem or some pedigree issue or his generally wild demeanor. I hate to speculate. It is indeed remarkable to see his Hummer with its license plate that has the little wheelchair on it, and the little wheelchair symbol hanging from his rearview mirror, but nobody utters the *remark*; not to Moose, anyway. You just wouldn't do that. Moose roars aimlessly and purposelessly all over the area, and he can go places where most people cannot. The locals have gotten used to seeing and hearing him careening down the road or uphill through the brush, or blasting through a stone wall. He is a "fixture," as one of our elderly friends says.

Anyway, that day when Moose saw that stalled vehicle and that helpless woman midstream, with clouds in the sky, rain likely, and light fading, he just naturally swooped down to her rescue. It was the thing to do.

In the lady's defense, this would admittedly involve the trembling of the earth, the debris cloud kicked up by Moose's Monster Hummer (rocks, mud, splintered trees, brush, trash, etc.), a flurry of flashing lights, and Moose's massive, six-foot-nine, overall-clad, hairy body emerging from the vortex of that tempest, roaring, "Grmphlink yrwmphld rkngpqx!" Which means, "What seems to be the trouble, Little Lady?" (It could be argued that Moose is somewhat inarticulate, when you first know him.) This is simply what the approach of Moose Vandergrift looks like. A simple fact of life.

That's about all Moose did, really: he went to her aid. Moose told me so. The "little lady" sent for her car from Fayetteville two full weeks later. Most people think she walked and crawled there, cross country, over some uncharted ATV trails that tunnel through the wilderness. Possibly barefooted. (Her shoes were there where she leaped out of them.) Sketchy details. There was some hair, some thread, a little blood. The dogs lost her scent somewhere in the national forest. She may have taken to the treetops, according to one experienced tracker. Terror is a great motivator. I say she had a panic attack. Others say that a panic attack doesn't last two weeks. I don't know.

From what I was able to gather from Moose personally, he "arrived," and he simply could not catch the lady. She screamed and hollered and took off up the riverbed waving her arms. Go figure. Moose tried to get her to stop by shouting to her as she fled. Anybody would have done that. But she was fast, and she was motivated, and the more he called to her the faster she ran. Moose told me so—at least, I think that's what he was saying.

Moose towed the car into town and fixed it, right there by the historic county jail. Then he went back and got his Hummer, which, by then, was in two feet of water. I say *that* was panic, too. Running off like that, the lady most likely frightened my buddy Moose—otherwise he would have used the Hummer to tow the car, or maybe to catch up with the woman. The situation just sorta snowballed, know what I mean? The sheriff commented on the teeth marks on the "come-along" cable Moose hooked to that axel, and on how a "normal" guy might have found another way. It should be mentioned also that it was just a small car.

Anyway, the lady swore to hospital officials and law enforcement authorities in Fayetteville that she had become lost, had had car trouble, and had encountered Bigfoot. Preposterous, I say. I know Moose, and Moose is not Bigfoot. Double-Dog Darrell knows Bigfoot, and he says Bigfoot is not Moose. The sheriff smoothed the whole thing over somehow, and all is well, although that particular lady does not vacation in our parts anymore.

Have I mentioned that Moose is my friend? He doesn't let anybody harm me. I am his mahoot, and I say he just takes a little getting used to.

GREETINGS

The Tuesday pool sessions (mini-tournaments, really) at the Senior Center became important to me once I turned myself in and admitted my age. I needed to "belong" somewhere. I had shot pool before, a lifetime ago, but this was new to me. Experienced, tough pool shooters! These guys, I hoped, were going to be my "buddies," and I wanted things to go right.

Right from the beginning, all of the guys smiled when I came into the room. I liked that, and I felt welcome: as if they had taken me under their wing. But I took note of the greetings proffered by each of them upon entering the pool room, and of the responses of the shooters present.

"What's up, Fellas?" was Old Hobson's greeting.

About eight pool cues would point at the ceiling, and someone would say, "That way." And, of course, it is important, if you ever expect to be any good at pool, to know which way is up.

"How ya doin'?" was the greeting of one of the volunteer pool competition organizers.

"Hanging on for dear life," was the response. "Just trying not to lose any ground. Just hangin' in there..." That sort of thing.

But always a reply. Something wise. If you said simply, "Hello. How are you today?" someone would say, "Well, I have this pain right up here under this rib, and I can't decide whether it's gas or just boredom with you guys' company." And that might go on to other physical ailments, doctor's appointments, surgery, and the high cost of pharmaceuticals, and the Veteran's Administration's campaign to kill off World War II guys and just get it over with. Perhaps a round of scar gazing.

When someone said, "How are you?" to me, I said, "Alive and

well. Well, alive." Nobody ever laughed, and that itself was the joke. The new guy didn't get laughs.

One man always shook everyone's hand and said, "Makin' it okay?" and then another of our bunch would always say, "With both hands and both feet." What that meant I cannot imagine. The remark always "laid there like a dead carp."

It seemed to me that someone ought to come up with an imaginative, colorful new greeting exchange. I suddenly understood the elaborate handshakes of the black guys back in the city: it was interesting and potentially full of meaning. I never did suggest that we have a secret handshake, though. I know what they would have told me to do with that idea.

"So, what's happenin'?" a late comer might say.

"Well, the planet is warming. Greenhouse gases are building in the atmosphere, and there's a hole in the ozone layer..."

"Oh, shut up."

"Well, that's what's happening. You asked."

All right, maybe the pool shooters didn't have much sincerity or diplomacy. Maybe they just couldn't give each other a break. Maybe this was going to be "guy stuff" for me from now on. When you got a response, you knew they saw you come into the room. If they bothered with wisecracks, you belonged.

"What are you fellas up to?" an arriving Harrison guy would ask innocently.

From all around the tables would come, "Oh, about five eleven...about six one...about five foot six now—used to be six foot..." Painful.

The Harrison guys were vicious. One of them would come in and announce, "Today I whip everybody!" And his buddy would say, "If you whip me, you walk home." Twenty miles.

A simple, "Good afternoon, gentlemen" would provoke a response of, "Gentlemen? Any of you guys a gentleman?"

One guy came in and said, "Greetings, my friends." And his best friend, really, but a joker like everybody else, said, "Friends? You only talk to your friends? What about me? Am I chopped liver here?"

Invariably, there was needling. "You're late. Couldn't get away from the wife, huh? What happened? She make you do the dishes?" Or, "Well! We thought you forgot. Have you got that whatchamacallit disease?" Or, "Come in here and take it like a man. You will have to fake it. Your wife told me so. Last night."

And everyone had insulting excuses for being there. "My wife brought me at gunpoint," or "It was this or soap operas," or "I just wanted to be near something level," or "All the decent people are busy and I had to come here," or "I missed my ride to the marathon yard sale tour," or "I won't be there with you guys in Hell, so I guess if I want to see you at all…"

***

Only one person could come through the door and simply wave, or chirp a sincere greeting, or flip out one of those rhetorical questions, and get away with it. Me. When I came in, nobody heard what I said. They just smiled broadly, or they shook my hand and told me how glad they were to see me. They asked me how I felt and whether I was staying all afternoon or not. I alone could bring joy to the room. I felt special, even blessed. These men liked to see me coming through the door.

Because in that room, everybody could beat me down like a dog.

I was their hope of not getting "skunked" in the day's pool session and having the little stuffed skunk tossed out on the table to add to the disgrace. (They named it after me.) I was insurance against humiliation.

Still, I had a role to play. I belonged. I was needed. Life was good.

Art by Scott Baldassari.

SHOWDOWN IN THE BERRY PATCH

All morning long, I had been working on my left hand. It's okay, if you are in a non-critical situation, to one-hand it, but if you are ever going to "make it" in berry-picking, you have got to be ambidextrous. I knew I was just too dependent upon my right hand, so I was in my secret blackberry patch that day deliberately picking with my left—a matter of necessity, even urgency.

Then *he* showed up. Rocko.

Oh, I knew it was him as soon as I saw his rig. Others would have known him by the crooked little pipe he held clenched in his teeth—or by his oily old felt hat with its band of braided garlic. Others would know his heavy eyebrows. And his North Dakota accent would tip others. Me? I recognized his cut-down, half-gallon Hiland (2%) milk container—its loop handle run through by a belt that slung it low on his hip like a holster. It was the perfect berry bucket, and it was just like one of mine. The one on the right. (Lately I had been packin' two!)

Rocko had been my unintentional mentor, really. We both were packing the half-gallon jug because he had taught me that trick in better, simpler times. I couldn't go the garlic thing, but I knew it was for repelling bugs. His shirt had long sleeves, too—for the thorns. He had taught me a lot. But that was back before he knew that I would be a rival picker, before our feud, before Limestone Valley.

Limestone. Some scars are deep and ugly and permanent. Limestone was a long time ago, and both of us had since looted berry patches from Log Hall to the Low Gap Mall and back again. We had taken gallons and gallons of every kind of wild berry out there, and we were both at the top of our game. But we had issues: with each other.

I locked my eyes on his. My little flat hat took care of the sun. (Funny how your hat starts smelling like cotton candy after a morning in the blackberries.) The brim of Roscoe's oily old felt hat was low, but his eyes blazed like a couple of blow torches. I let the heel of my right hand brush the top of my berry bucket, and I squared my shoulders. I was ready; and I knew Rocko: he was always ready.

Truth be told, I was a little beat up at that moment. I had several chigger bites still nagging me—from back in raspberry season. Below the cliffs two turns north of Scenic Point, I had picked up a two-inch scratch on my left forearm. And then there was that sliver from McElroy Gap! Yeah, I was hurting. But I wasn't going to let *him* know that.

***

"It's been a long time, Rocko," I said calmly.

"Not long enough."

"Yeah. I was in no hurry for this. I had enough of you at Limestone Valley."

"Limestone! That was a long time ago."

"Not long enough."

It was always like that with us: sharp, clever repartee, and then trouble. We eyeballed each other and circled to our right.

"We both picked a lot of berries out there," I snarled, screwing my face into a menacing sneer that I myself could not have faced from the other side. "But then you got greedy!"

"Did not."

"Did, too."

"Did not."

"You stole a quart of my black raspberries out there—right out of my pick-up."

"I did not. I wouldn't want your sorry berries. You don't pick clean enough."

Well, that hurt. I was always a clean picker (not a leaf or a bug or a green berry anywhere in my bucket), and by now Rocko knew it. He was just trying to change the subject, knock me back a little, pull my chain. He knew how to hurt me.

"You lie like a rug, Old Man." (He was four years older than I was, and I knew he hated that.)

"Are you calling me a liar?"

"You're quick. We were the only pickers in the woods, and someone stole a quart of my berries, and I say it was you!"

We paused, reversed our pattern, and circled to the left. But that didn't last. Rocko stopped dead and spread his legs, his boots planted firmly in the dry clay, fully 32 inches apart, maybe 33. At his height, I wondered how he kept his balance. He faced me now, his right hand dangerously near his Hiland milk jug.

"Are you calling me a thief?"

"Well, let me see: I twice accused you of stealing my berries, rather plainly, I thought. And I said you lied, and I called you Old Man. Yeah: old liar and old thief. I did that. If the shoe fits..."

"Then I call you one right back, because someone nailed a half-gallon of my berries that day in Limestone Valley, and the way I figure it, that was you!"

Taken aback, I began circling to my left again, after a little stutter step to my right. And Rocko went off balance! He was over-extended, I could see that. A man's gotta know his limitations. Rocko staggered clumsily, and nearly fell. I steadied him. (A reflex.)

But the beauty of the milk jug berry bucket is that you can stumble around like that and not lose berries. That had been Rocko's breakthrough invention, his contribution to Mankind, his artful device! He recovered without dropping one berry, and he faced me.

"Right back at yuh," he snarled. "Thief and liar!"

"Wait a minute," I said. "You lost berries out there, too?"

"I did."

"But if you were robbed, and I was robbed, and we both lost berries..."

Things went quiet. The sun glinted on the rim of his berry bucket, and my glasses bounced an annoying light into his eyes. Both of us were thinking, remembering.

"Could be there was somebody else out there in that berry brush," Rocko said finally. "Just once, I thought I heard somethin'— a little song, tinkley-like."

"You heard that, too? I thought it was you—on a cell phone!"

"What is a cell phone?" I knew he knew what a cell phone was, but he was telling me he didn't have one. Hmmm.

***

Grimly, we stared at each other for a long moment. Then we realized that, really, we ought to be friends. We stood there, ready for anything—tense, coiled like springs, crouched like panthers, focused like lasers. In both of our minds, the replay of the Limestone thing spun through. Could we be wrong? Could both of us be wrong? I had heard that sound, too, but you hear a lot of things in the berry brush. Could we have been so preoccupied with the berries and with watching each other that we were blindsided by someone else? These things are never simple. We should have known.

Finally, it was Rocko who broke. "I didn't mean to say that you didn't pick clean."

That helped a lot. "And I didn't mean it when I called you a liar and a thief. I could have been wrong," I said.

"And old. You said old."

"Sorry about that, too."

"Understandable mistake, I guess. And I have thought the same about you—all this time."

"Coulda been kids," I said, "with that phone."

"Yeah. They got no respect. Coulda been kids."

"Coulda been government, too." Nobody hereabouts trusts the government—much.

"Yeah. Woods is full o' *them*."

***

Well, we patched that one up. It was close there—could have been messy. It took time, but eventually it blew over. We just let it drop. Rocko and I play Bingo together now—down at the Legion Hall with our wives. I work my cards left-handed, and Rocko has noticed. Someday we may figure out the Limestone Valley thing, and someday we might pick the same berry patch together again. Next summer, maybe. Raspberries. These things take time.

Now that I think about it, though, there are a couple of tricks I want to show Rocko: things I learned on my own on a rocky shelf just below the Cliff House Restaurant in a snag of treacherous blackberry brush near the mouth of a cave. But I've gotta let it out slow—one thing at a time—and I've gotta make him wait.

Yeah. Next summer.

THERE GOES THE NEIGHBORHOOD

No, Son, you got it all wrong. I don't think you was a-payin' attention to what I was a-sayin'. That boy is your relative. No two ways about it."

I was having it out with one of the locals down at the café. Old Rathbone, whom some called a know-it-all, was trying to get through to me, and I was trying to listen to him because I liked his indelible image. He was a transplant, too, but he had come up the mountain thirty years ago, and he was almost native.

"Quit yer snickerin' at me, and listen," he said, "cuz I know what I'm a-talkin' about here."

He had a blue bandana tight on his skull—no hair in sight— and a long white beard, narrow and pointing at his navel (I hope). He was crusty, and I wouldn't have it any other way. Rather a ruddy complexion: wind hardened. The waitresses liked him because they could wrap him around their little fingers. He was one of those paper tigers you hear about. Or a big Teddy Bear. And a good tipper.

"Son, when someone lives a mile away, that's a good neighbor; when he lives a half a mile away, he's a neighbor; when he lives a quarter of a mile away, that's pushin' things. But this guy you've got on yer mountain? Well, hell, that's a relative! That's a law."

***

Wifey and I had tried to buy the parcel of land adjacent to ours. We had written letters and made phone calls and offered money. We even argued that we were every local's dream: Big City Texans who would pay too much money for land. It was indeed a family thing in the end, though. The owner sold the land to a relative of his. Then the clear-cutting proceeded: the land was logged to within an inch of its life, right there at the end of our clothesline. And then it was re-sold, this time to someone who wanted clear land to build on.

"All he wants to do is build a house with a view—like ours," I told Wifey.

"Yeah, right."

Well, I was right. The new owner built, and he built so close that we could hear him sneeze the first time the pollen count went up. We could hear the clink of glasses and china at meal time. We could hear whole conversations. At night, we didn't dare listen.

We had moved out of a city where the neighbors were "in our face" and we were in theirs. We had both lived in apartments where they were above us and below us, in front of us and in back of us, and to both sides—all shapes, sizes, and colors. We had listened to people just through the walls fighting or making love or partying down. And we had gotten together and escaped all of that at first opportunity.

Now this guy was out there in the boonies with us, just like we were, well, relatives.

***

"You mark my words: this man's got to be kin," said Rathbone. "Who else would want to live that close to anybody? The mountains is full of quiet, secluded places. I can take you to places that varmints is afraid to go—a half mile from yer house. Anybody moves in that close to you's got to be a relative! You sure this guy ain't yer son or yer first cousin or some damn thing?"

"I am certain. He's a nice fellow, and he has a nice wife, but I've checked it out, and they are definitely not family."

"I bet they're yer wife's family then." He moved close to me. Too close. Rathbone was one of those personal space invaders.

"Not a chance."

"But they cain't do that! They's rules about things like this. When they got the whole damn mountain, they ain't no reason to move into yer dooryard. Where they from?"

"A city," I said, backing off a little.

"A city where?"

"It doesn't make any difference. Evidently, they want to live like they did in the city: right on top of us."

"Lonesome folks." He leaned closer to me, and I leaned away.

"Well, I don't know about that. Fact is, they have every right to build right where they built and live right where they live, and we're just stuck with it."

"Son, you got urban sprawl right in yer yard. But I betcha somp'n, Son: I bet if you got on the Internet and dug around, you'd find that boy has yer blood runnin' in his veins." He was, by then, advancing, and I was backing up.

"He's not Danish, not Norwegian, not Swede. I already checked."

"He's white, ain't he? And you're white."

"Lots of people are white, but they're not all my relatives. I'm not even sure all of my relatives are white." I got some furniture between us.

"I bet you six bits that boy is yer cousin or somp'n."

"No way."

***

Well, that went on for a while. So, I went to the Internet and scoped them out, scoped out my family tree, looked for my neighbor in the limbs of both of our family trees. Wifey had some American Indian in her—Cherokee—and so this mountain was really more her neighborhood than mine. (Imagine a casino next door! There are relatives and there are relatives!) But no, my closest neighbor was not our kin. It was pretty much official. Next time at the café, I reported my findings to Old Rathbone, rather smugly I must admit.

"If they ain't yer blood relatives, Son, you got to do somethin' drastic. You don't want no scandals."

"Certainly it can't be that bad," I said weakly.

Wifey was far more concerned about the situation than I. She was forever procuring seedlings and putting them into the sparse remains of the woods between us and our new neighbors.

She even considered bamboo. I concentrated on minding my own business—blotting it all out with my mind. I wasn't going to be permitted to be buddies with the neighbor guy, so I decided to be silent, "distant," if you will. But Old Rathbone kept at us.

"They's talk goin' around. You can't be a-livin' up there with them folks unless you can prove they're your kin." He was in my space again.

"Sure we can," I told him, dancing back. "Look at this. This is us living with these strangers right in our mutual yard. We're doing it. Hello." (I saw that on TV. I don't talk that way to real people, usually.)

"Well, then one of you has got to marry one of *them*. It's the onliest decent thing to do."

"Oh no we don't," said Wifey. "*This* marriage is enough. Get out of my face."

"I mean it," argued Rathbone. "It could be illegal, immoral, or somethin' worse! Tell you what: why don't you folks *adopt* them neighbors of yours!"

"What?"

"Take out a bunch o' papers—get some signatures, have a judge bang one of them little hammers. Adopt them folks and get this cancer out of your lives. They need to be relatives." He was not moving toward either of us anymore.

"That is so not-going-to-happen," said Wifey. (Wifey learned that on TV, too—from a dog.)

"Then you got to move," said Old Rathbone thoughtfully. "I don't see no other way."

"Look," I said, "Don't you think that you have interpreted a rather colorful local axiom a bit too literally here?"

"Say what?" He actually backed up!

"Well, the law or fundamental principle you have cited seems to be predicated on a gross exaggeration—hyperbole, if you will—and circuitous logic. What these sages mean to say is that a second dwelling built in close proximity to an existing home in this neighborhood USUALLY belongs to one of the offspring—a phenomenon possibly dating back to European or British tradition—NOT that if such a structure is built it must house blood relatives as a matter of statute law." I advanced toward *him* on that.

"Gettin' mighty uppity, ain't we! Well, y'awl kin set there and argue and use new fangled big words if'n you want to, but I cain't be seen around nobody who's a-livin' out of wedlock and probably in a state of terrible sin with people they don't like and don't even know. I got to distance myself from sich things. It would be different if you lived in town. I got places to go and things to do." And Old Rathbone abandoned us, right there: actually went away mad!

***

As we see it, the only thing to do is play the TV loud to drown out the neighbors, and plant trees. In summer we get the help of extra leaves on the trees to block the line of sight, and katydids, cicadas, and tree frogs—white noise, like traffic, airplanes, and gunfire in the city—to mask the conversations. In view of Rathbone's last remark about reputation and sin and his interpretation of the local code, and especially the "in town" phrase, I have considered looking into filing "a bunch o' papers," and turning the mountaintop into an incorporated village. People can live close to each other in town without violating any laws. It's too late for other solutions. (Wifey would be mayor, of course.)

We want to get along with our real neighbors, who are at least 440 yards away.

THE FINEST PEOPLE IN THE WORLD

We were up at Old Hooper's place, a mountain or two over, and Wifey and I were helping our old buddy enjoy the cool of his shade trees. Sometimes, he assured us, it was so good he needed help with it. It was July, and there had been very little rain, and we were all sweating that year's garden.

"I don't expect it will rain now until after Labor Day," our host moaned. "It ain't fair. I don't have no luck. If it was a-rainin' hundred dollar bills, I'd be a-settin' in jail!" He was just mildly disgusted.

"Oh, it'll rain," said Wifey. "Just hang in there—but get out the hose, too."

"If it was a-rainin' soup, I'd be a-settin' there with a fork!"

"It will rain. Just keep watering, and hope."

"Yeah, gotta save that sweet corn."

"I haven't had good sweet corn since I left Nebraska," I offered.

"Nebraska?" said Old Hooper. "You lived in Nebraska?"

"You bet. With college, I lived there for about ten years."

"Finest people in the world live in Nebraska. Spent some time there myself. Cornhuskers, they call themselves. Fine folks."

"I loved those people. I lived in a Czech community: duck and dumplings, sauerkraut, kolaches. And lots to drink."

"I thought you lived in Iowa," Wifey said.

"That was high school."

"Ioway?" said Old Hooper. "They's no finer people anywhere than in Ioway. Hawkeyes! And all that beef!"

"Yeah: corn fed beef and Sioux Bee Honey and the best pork anywhere. The Amana Colony! Great feasting there. I miss Iowa and Nebraska."

"We're doing fine right here. I like that big cloud over there. Looks promising." Wifey was being the optimist.

"Yep: Iowa beef—out of Omaha! And corn up to the sky! My God! Finest people anywhere," said Old Hooper. He stretched and cast an eye toward his weedless garden nearby. "Of course, I'm from southern Illinois myself. Great folks there, too."

"Been there," I said, "and you're right. Wonderful people. Had some trouble on the road there, and they saved me like I was their own—and wouldn't take a dime. Bailed me out. Fed me like I was family."

"Yep. Best people around."

For a while, we kicked back and just breathed. There was a breeze, and a puff of cooler air. Old Hooper was eighty -eight years old at the time, still heavily into his gardening, his mind alive and full of memories—and compassion.

"I thought I heard a little rumble over that way," Wifey said.

"Nope. It ain't Labor Day yet. Probably just an airplane."

"I think I got into some bean soup along that road in southern Illinois that was the best I ever had," I murmured. I closed my eyes and just received the coolness. This was a good time, and I knew it. A lazy, comfortable, promising day. "I was rolling along in the dead of night, and I saw this Bean Soup sign, and I stopped. Memorable soup."

"I thought you said you was from Minnesody," said Old Hooper.

"Well, I was! Born and raised most of the way, right up there in the cold. Todd County. I can't seem to get back there. They call themselves Minnesotazens now. But that's God's Country up there."

"Finest people on Earth live in Minnesody. Toughest ones live there year round. I used to fish there of a summer, but I wouldn't go there in the winter." Old Hooper actually shivered about there. And I remember a little chill myself, just thinking about Minnesota in February.

"Ice fishing. They go in for ice fishing. Freeze your butt. And your toes."

"I think it's going to rain," said Wifey.

"Naw. It's just foolin' with us. Won't rain till after Labor Day. Just a bad year."

"We used to eat the heck out of those bluegills and northerns when I was a kid, and then there was the sucker run in the Spring. They used to spear them illegally at night and smoke 'em. Good stuff." I don't know. I guess I was just hungry.

"I heard another rumble," said Wifey.

"Jist the wind."

"I had friends who went over and picked up potatoes in the fields in the Red River valley between Minnesota and the Dakotas. Sacked them in the fields. Long time ago."

"Some of the finest people anywhere are those Dakota folks. North Dakota, South Dakota. Nothin' lonlier than a North Dakota wheat farmer. Nobody out there."

"Ever eat with a threshing crew, Hooper? On the old-fashioned threshing machine where you pitched bundles and all that?"

"My God, yes. We ate like the Amish, and worked like 'em, too. Out there in all that wheat and oats."

"Tables out under the trees at the edge of the fields, just groaning with food: six or seven kinds of meat, ten or so vegetables, watermelon. The women brought it all out there at noon. What a pig-out. I got in on that myself when I was a kid. That was before Diet Coke." I remembered it well.

"Finest women in the world, them farm wives."

"I think I felt a drop."

"Ioway, Minnesody, Nebraska, Illinois, the Dakotas…Missouri folks, too, and of course, us Arkansawyers!"

"And Texas," I said. "You take the Lopez Mexican Restaurant in Southwest Houston? Best Tex-Mex food there ever was or is ever apt to be. Wonderful salza."

"And folks," said Hooper. "Them East Texas folks is among the best on Earth. They cain't help it. Ever time they open their mouths, they pour out warmth and charity and all the God-given virtues."

"I love East Texas," I said.

"New York!" said Wifey.

"Whaaat?"

"New York. Long Island. Port Jeff."

"Oh, yeah. Finest people ever was. Some of them New York boys and me shot up a mess of them Kamikazes back when Mr. Roosevelt sent us all on vacation together in the Pacific Ocean. Fine soldiers come outa New York."

"I love New York. Nathan's hot dogs, all that Times Square pizza you can just reach in off the street and grab. Best deli joints on Earth. Best junk food in the Universe."

"Outer Mongolia," blurted Wifey.

"Whaaat?"

"Finest people in the world," she said. "Now let's get inside. I don't know if you've noticed, but it's raining."

"My God. Must be Labor day."

BARNEY'S DAY OFF

Poor Barney Kleggler had become one of those small, gray husband/props you sometimes notice ditched on a bench near the doors at Wal-Mart. He had been a drooling "doofus" for years before I met him: a joke among men, infamous down at the feed store, in area barber shops, at ad hoc "county meetings," wherever men gathered.

He had been taken over, the way people in science fiction movies get taken over by pod creatures or implanted computer chips—just emptied of his spirit, his will, his very soul.

That was the Barney I had seen being steered around town: pressed blue jeans, shiny penny loafers, sometimes a light blue shirt and crooked necktie. I wondered about him, and the guys shooting pool at the 'Center filled me in. The pool players, all noble men, did not normally gossip, but I asked, and they were my friends by then. They told me Barney had traded away everything for "a little peace and quiet," and had made a horribly bad deal—sadder still because he had once been a man of force and had headed up a company that employed a hundred people and produced some whimsical, imaginative products.

Some said it started when he lost control of the TV remote there in their living room. But the theory among the pool players was that the trouble really started when Barney's wife impulsively took over the driving just after his retirement from his company, maybe to do him a favor. (Retirement was the definite pivot point and the key word, for sure.) "He just handed her the car keys one day," someone said, "and after that, she was in charge." It was not long before his skills were gone and he supposedly could not drive at all. Then he just let his license lapse, then his brain.

Very soon, he could not handle the plumbing, electrical, structural, mechanical, and aesthetic problems around the house and grounds that the rest of us retirees in the mountains must handle ourselves. Barney listened as his shortcomings or failures became source material for comic phone conversations between his wife and her friends as they discussed their pathetic husbands. (I have been told by other men that some wives do that. I could not accuse Wifey of such behavior. I insist.)

Soon, everything Barney said or did or thought drew criticism, and so he stopped saying and doing and thinking anything; then his wife credited him with things he did not remember having said or done or thought, and angrily screamed at him about all of it. His facial expressions drew criticism, too (he had to explain every smile and frown), and so he developed a completely blank expression—which made his wife even more angry. He responded with further withdrawal, and he turned his mind into a blank page. That was the concensus scuttlebutt, anyway—among the "boys."

Barney's wife eventually had to take over everything he ate, drank, spent, wore, saw, or heard. It just snowballed. His gait degraded to a shuffle, then a mince: little, choppy, six-inch steps. He became a zombie, a slug, an inert mass, and he stood around with a *VACANCY* sign on his forehead, his arms just dangling there from his narrow shoulders like two nailed-on boards. She led him around by the hand. Everybody noticed, and most just looked away. Senility, they thought.

"One time she hid his false teeth until the sweet corn was all gone," I heard someone say over a game of pool . I have no confirmation of that report. I had heard that said of other couples on other occasions. I wouldn't repeat that with much confidence. Probably just a lame joke.

According to one of the great thinkers around the pool table, "He didn't stand his ground. He just quit. A man like that—who ran things until the day he retired! He turned himself into a puddle of jelly and his wife walked the puddle dry."

Barney withdrew from life and became preoccupied with

stroking smooth, varnished woodwork surfaces. His eyes did not focus. He was through.

***

One bright and sunny day I slipped out the back door of the Senior Center just after lunch while Wifey was preoccupied with some sort of project. I dashed across the street to a small shopping center—four or five small shops constructed to look like a slice of Main Street USA at Disney World: flags, banners, lamp posts, plenty of color. I needed a real Diet Coke, and I knew they had one in that one little shop.

But there was Poor Barney, sitting on the curb by a little push-cart, almost totally limp. At first I thought it was some sort of dummy. He reminded me of a puppet whose strings had been snipped. And those arms just hung there. Disturbing.

"Are you okay, Barney?" I asked, approaching tentatively.

He said nothing. He did not move at all. I went over for a closer look, and when he shifted his eyes, I was so startled I jumped back.

"You okay there, Barney? Something I can do for you?" I didn't know what to do, but I had to say something. We had never had an extended conversation.

Barney said nothing. He followed me with his eyes, though, so I knew he was alive, sorta, and I started backing away toward the door of the little shop. Maybe someone would have to make some calls. Someone else. But then there was a sudden move.

"I have an idea!" Barney said loudly. "I have an enormous idea!" He stood up.

"Whaat?" I went close to him again.

"I have a rip-roaring idea! My wife is gone, and I have an idea!"

"Gone? Your wife is gone?" Right away, I was worried. She was nowhere around, and from all reports he had long since become completely dependent upon her. What had happened? The car she always drove him around in was nowhere nearby. He was indeed there alone.

"They're having a Woman Meeting somewhere today, making plans and scheming. I got loose. I am alone. I am free."

"Oh. Well, are you okay? I mean, congratulations and all that, but you are okay, aren't you?" It was as if I had found an errant Alzheimer's patient or someone escaped from a mental ward somewhere, or a newly awakened Rip Van Winkle.

"Never better," said Poor Barney, standing straighter. Then he actually shook his arms and legs and did some preliminary stretching exercises and I stood there with my mouth open. He rotated his neck a little, cracked his knuckles, flexed his knees.

"Well, good," I said, retreating toward the door of the little shop. (If I could just get inside, I would be out of this scene.)

"Wait," said Barney. "I have always admired you and your opinion. Can I run my idea past you?"

"Me? Gee, I suppose so. Nobody ever asks me for my opinion. Wifey handles most of that sort of thing these days."

"Be careful about that," he said. Then he asked, "This is your store, isn't it?"

"My store? Oh no—I don't own this. I live out south on the mountain. Retired."

"Oh, I thought you were the owner. I guess it was the sun glasses."

The owner of the store is a very handsome man with an athletic build and a great winning smile. He owns many things in town, and he does what it is almost impossible to do: he makes a living right there in the town! He is brilliant and talented, and he is committed to the town. I could not fathom the misidentification, sunglasses or no.

"Well, you say you have an idea. I do like ideas. Go ahead and run it by me—if you wish."

"Well, I don't know. You say you don't own this—you're retired?"

"Yeah. I was a school teacher, and so I like ideas. I love ideas— especially rip-roaring ones. I write a little these days."

I had to talk Barney into telling me about his scheme. He said the little store fired his imagination because of all the wild stuff it had for sale. He had made a good living making novelty items in his day. I had not been a businessman—but I had always been interested in how such places worked. I did not try to convince him that I was worthy of his confidence, but I promised to be worthy of his trust. In other words, I would keep my mouth shut.

"Well, " he said, "You were a teacher, and that's bad, but I like your hat. So maybe you qualify a little."

This was already more than Poor Barney and I had said to each other in all the time I had known him. He had been a single-syllable guy around me: Yup, Nope, Ooops, Darn. And he had a short moan going when his wife barked a command, sometimes. I had tried being gushy once, but that was just once long ago. We were not buddies. But now we were going to have an actual exchange.

"I got to thinking once a while back when I was with my wife shopping. If I had sort of a prayer rug along, I could get right down on my knees and beg her to go home." Abrupt like that.

"A prayer rug."

"Well, sort of a pleading rug. You know how it is when they get into a shopping mode: they won't go home. If we had a pad, we could comfortably kneel right down on and plead with them to come out of the store and go home. You see what I mean?"

"Most husbands..."

"Exactly. Most husbands. You would make this mat or rug, see, and a guy could just have it along, and after about ten or twelve hours of marathon shopping, he could just practically prostrate himself and humbly supplicate..."

"A pleading mat!" I exclaimed. "I think I like this."

Poor Barney brightened and smiled, and I had never seen that before. Not personally. There were stories. I was impressed.

"Well, not so fast," he said. "Now, it would be very cynical to offer this product as what it actually was, see what I mean? I mean, this would make most women, especially wives, somewhat angry, and they would come out swinging—sink their fangs in your throat, rip you to shreds, beat you down like a mongrel dog, pound you to a pile of..."

"I'm with you…"

"So you gotta call it something else. And I think I've got that figured, too."

"Go on."

"Well, I was watching my wife in the garden. She doesn't can or freeze anything, but she likes to grow vegetables—and flowers. But I saw *her* on *her* knees, you see."

"Begging the plants to grow…"

"No! She was weeding. But I thought, if she had a rug or mat or something, it would be easier on her knees, and I put the two ideas together, and I think I have a product!"

"A knee-saving garden mat!"

"Yeah, but *men* could use it in their own special way, and get away with buying it because of the garden thing. I could open a booth at a flea market, put them up for sale online, get them into some stores, maybe eventually hook up with Wal-Mart, then Neiman-Marcus…"

"You're a genius, Barney! I think your idea is a winner." A little enthusiasm on my part.

"It could be real carpet," Barney thought out loud, "or it could be foam rubber or woven plastic of some kind. And it could be cute—like an animal face, or an enemy's face, or a mushroom or a stone or something natural. But all of the men, you see, would recognize it for what it was, and the wives would just think it was a good garden aid. Make me some money, by God!" Barney actually pranced a little about there—I swear it.

I tried to add upbeat additions to his concept, but I had to ask him about the obvious problem. The first time a guy used the mat for pleading purposes—in the wife's girlfriend's driveway, at the thrift shop, at a shoe store or dress shop, at a nursery or garden center, etc. (wherever women can't tear themselves away from), the game would be over. Women have an inscrutable network. They have meetings, as Barney pointed out.

"By the time they catch on and put out a hit," said the businessman, "I will have made a small fortune."

"You're absolutely right, sir, and I want to invest," I said, just as if I had money to toss in there.

"Can't let you do that," he said. "I've got the capital covered. But thanks. I'll be sending you a nice consulting fee."

Then Barney, who had been pacing about and using his hands, indeed his whole body, to get his point across, suddenly froze. I looked where he was looking, and sure enough, his wife was driving past. The car slowed and started jockeying into a quick U-turn.

"Quick," said Barney, "lead me over to that lamp post. She's spotted me." He dropped his arms to their accustomed position, he shrunk before my eyes and pulled up into a knot, his eyes glazed over, and I led him delicately over to the lamp post. He used those tiny, mincing steps, he staggered a little, and he trembled.

"Why?" I whispered.

"Later," he said quietly.

I leaned him against the post there, and then I helped load him into the car, and his wife smiled wanly and thanked me, buckled Barney's seat belt, and drove off. I stood there for a long time, stunned and strangely exhausted.

And now I'm stuck wondering how many husbands there are out there like Barney—playing possum. And what will happen the next time she takes her eye off him—for a Woman Meeting or something! I keep thinking he is going to break loose and make a ton of money! I don't know anything about business, but I do like ideas. And I want one of those mats.

THE STORY BEHIND THE STORY

Any absence from the local scene, once Wifey and I were established in our adopted mountain community, left us disoriented and uninformed, almost certainly misinformed. It was best for us to return from any extended trip and quickly jump into community events with both feet, and with very open minds.

The Friends of the Library's annual Watermelon Seed Spitting Contest was raging away in the village square when we hit town, and, naturally, Wifey and I could not miss that. We had been out of pocket for a full week—off mountain, out of state, back to Texas, into the city for opera and old friends and "theatah." This event would serve nicely to get us plugged back in.

Dr. Schullenheimer was the head judge, and several dignitaries from around the county were present, and the contestants were all enthusiastic. All-American refreshments were at hand, bunting on the gazebo, the whole nine yards! Somewhere a band was playing. It was an altogether festive occasion, well attended, and fraught with drama: the thrill of victory, and the agony of not being worth spit. Ideal.

We learned the rules, signed up as contestants, and started mingling; and, right away, I could tell that something wonderful had happened: something absolutely juicy! Wifey picked up on it, too, and soon we were both working the crowd with a purpose. There had been an incident! We started picking up fragments, then amusing details. Something scandalous had occurred!

The local paper, it seemed, had reported that a dispatcher at the county sheriff's office had been "let go" because of being found in a "compromising position" with a prisoner. But who? And whom? (The paper would be able to have only *a* story, but not *the* story. Political correctness and all that. They can't alienate people. Everybody is connected.) The full story, though, was there somewhere, at the Seed Spitting Contest, in the crowd. Wifey and I worked quickly.

My turn came, and I stepped up and spat my seeds, rather badly, received only polite applause, and then faded back into the crowd searching for the truth of the dispatcher story. I did not see how Wifey did when she competed.

I had previously learned that the farther from the general population a person lived, the better informed he was about local events, especially scandals. It seemed that people who were arguably hermits had the straight skinny on all gossip, rumors, scandals, lies and fabrications. So, I was relieved when I found Old Zeke Davidshoffer out at the edge of the seed spitting crowd.

Old Zeke lives alone, so far out in the woods, to hear him tell it, that mere social creatures like skunks, coons, deer, armadillos, and squirrels are afraid to go there. He lives with bears and mountain lions. And, of course, Bigfoot. He has no electricity, no phone lines, no close human neighbors. Rumor is that he "invented" himself decades ago to work as a character at Dogpatch USA, a hillbilly amusement park, now defunct. When Dogpatch died, he became the character he had portrayed: a strange, concocted creation.

According to our old neighbor lady, some of "these people" believe that, at nightfall, the darkness begins deep in the woods and creeps up out of the woods to swallow up roads and houses and barns, and eventually everything, and that's how night works! I asked her which people, and she told me I was an ass, and Wifey kicked me blue under the table. Go figure. Anyway, for my money, Old Zeke lives out there where that darkness she mentioned begins. The road dives off Highway 7, winds in and down and around and off, and finally just gives up and ends in a pile of rocks, deep deep in the woods. Zeke lives five hundred yards beyond that point. That qualifies him completely as an authority on local issues.

So, I knew Old Zeke would have the straight story, right? And I buttonholed him, pulled Wifey over to us, and asked Old Zeke the provocative question. It was like touching a fuse with a lighted match.

"Oh, the dispatcher thing! That's a good one," he said, his eyes bugging out like one of those terrorists we keep seeing on TV. He pulled us both away from a sudden outburst of riotous noise from the contest, and we sat down on the steps of the gazebo. "That's the best story ever was. But you tell me what you know first."

***

We knew very little, but we wanted to know everything: which of the four female dispatchers had gotten herself into a "compromising position," what constituted a "compromising position," what were they compromising about, who had seen what, and all the juicy details. There had been booze involved, supposedly: booze from the evidence lock-up! And danger! And sex! (I remembered sex from somewhere back in the Twentieth Century.) Someone had gone to the hospital! We needed details.

"The High Sheriff and his boys was out a-bustin' a meth lab," Old Zeke confided, moving close. "One of the deputies has a stool pigeon, you see—a highly secretive informant—who brings him information." Zeke drew me in closer, and whispered, "That would be Clarissa Snitch. She comes from a long line of them informers dating back to the Civil War."

"Big secret," I intoned.

"Terrible secret," Zeke said with a frown. He was all dressed up for town. It was summertime, and he had come a long way, and he was going to have to get home in all that darkness later. He was clad mostly in denim, and his slouch hat was brightly decorated with a hatband of l960's flavor. There was a hairy hunter/prospector/train robber air about him. What he had done at Dogpatch I could not imagine.

"All of them that cooperates with The Law is secretive types," he said. "Anyway, The High Sheriff and his merry band was out a-raidin' a Pullman car this one fella has a-settin' out here on a mountain. Don't know why he's got a Pullman car out there, but he's got one."

"Hey, I know where that thing is. Not a railroad in the county, either!"

"And they's nothin' in it, not a meth lab or a blade of forbidden grass or a pill or booze—nothin' interesting at all."

"I thought I heard they busted a meth lab out there," probed Wifey.

"That was before the story filtered through the woods and the lies was strained out. All them lies strains out between Highway 7 and my place, you know. The woods is a filter. There weren't nothin' in that Pullman car, and there still ain't—although you can sleep there if yer stuck far from home of a dark night.

"Anyways, The High Sheriff and his boys, you see, creep up on this Pullman car, surround it, and come a-blastin' in—only to find out the pathetic truth. Ain't nothin' in that Pullman car! So they packs up all their gear and heads back to the Historic Jasper Jail empty handed. And when they gets there, they immediately see that they got what they call a *sitchyashion*!"

***

Old Zeke slowed the whole thing down now, because he knew he had us. He pulled out a bottle of spring water. I know it was spring water, because it said so right on the bottle. I was not envious, because I had my own Diet Coke in hand. Mine brought no tears to my eyes, but his water seemed to do that to him. An emotional thing, maybe. Go figure.

Old Zeke continued after a healthy gulp from his water jug. "The dispatcher, a girl who had been fired from Wal-Mart, where she had worked at that return/exchange counter—where you bring back the stuff you bought by mistake?—for about six days. She was fired because they said she was too gullible—let some old lady bring back a bustle: one of them things women a hundred years ago or so used to make their hind ends look big. Paid her good money fer it. Someone else said she let somebody return a buffalo robe! Stuff Wal-Mart never sold, ever! Well, they fired her. And Wal-Mart is very good about handicapped workers."

"Anyway…" said Wifey impatiently.

"Anyways, this trustee—prisoner—had convinced that gullible girl to play a little game of Monopoly usin' the counterfeit money from the evidence lock-up, drinkin' the booze the sheriff had grabbed in a bust a few weeks back, and even usin' loaded dice they had there. And somehow, this turned out to be Strip Monopoly!"

"You don't mean it!"

"Musta been Strip Monopoly, 'cuz there was a lot of fumblin' around for clothes when the High Sheriff pranced in. And a lot of confusion, too, because that trustee somehow walked clean outa there while the boys was preoccupied with eyeballin' the female dispatcher, and helpin' her, and he took along a jug of vodka and the keys to the historic jail house."

"Was *he* naked?" I asked.

"No. Had on that orange outfit the prisoners get to wear. Guess they put out an APB about that—you think?"

"How'd he get the keys?" Wifey asked.

"Oh, they's lots o' copies of them keys knockin' around, but he jist picked up the ones he had been a-playin' with all evenin' and run off. O' course, he went home. All them escaped prisoners you hear about? They go home." Old Zeke made that part sound tender, even taking off his hat and clutching it to his breast. "They need the love," he said.

"So the Sheriff just went out and picked him up, right?" I have a knack for these things myself. I could see how the story was going.

"Yep. Just drove out to this feller's place, and there he was. But the High Sheriff gets hold of this mysterious jug that's a-settin' there, and he takes a whiff of it, and he passes slick and clean out. So, guess what? They'd found themselves a real meth lab this time, and they had to drag the sheriff off to the hospital."

"Good lord."

"Well, I should hope. That's what happened, I'm pretty sure. Anyways, it's a-getting' dark out there, and it's time to arrest the trustee again, and the trustee jist takes them keys and heads fer the woods. Well, a deputy yells at him, but he won't stop because he can't hear nothin' over the tree frogs and katydids and cicadas that's yammerin' in the woods. You know, I think them things must all be deef, cuz all that racket is matin' calls, and they don't seem to hear each other a-callin'. They yell all night long. Ever night in July and on into August! You'd think they'd hear that racket and pop up and say, 'Here I am—let's boogy' or somethin'."

"Well, how did the deputies arrest that guy?" Wifey wanted to get back on task.

"One of them fired a shot in the air. And now, here's the part that I find suspicious. A big owl comes a-plummetin' down out of the sky and hits the High Sheriff on the head. Now, I say it was the fumes that knocked him out—from that jug?—but some say it was really the owl, and somebody made up the part about them fumes."

"Someone thinks the owl falling out of the sky is more believable than the fume story?" (I have a skepticism about such things. I have instincts.)

"Well, it's a better story. Old Hobson heard it was a goose, but he never gets it straight. Anyways, the sheriff went to the hospital, the prisoner went back to jail, a big meth lab got broke up, and the dispatcher got fired. And you was in the city a-wastin' *your* time when it all went down." Old Zeke drank to his own summation.

Old Zeke leaned out of one side of the gazebo, maybe just a little "hydrated" by the contents of his personal water jug, and preached to the crowd. "All the baddies is in jail, and the innocent and the naive roam free. Say Amen!" Nobody seemed to know what that had to do with seed spitting.

About that time, there was a roar from the considerable crowd. A man from Louisiana (recently transplanted to the area) had spat a seed so far nobody believed their eyes. Doc Schullenheimer confirmed it, though, measuring it scientifically, examining the seed and the deed. It was a great effort, and the man was later awarded the trophy for his age group. If he was from inside the town, he could have run for mayor—and won. But it turned out that he was "rim folk" now—a near neighbor to Wifey and me up on the mountain.

***

We heard other versions of the dispatcher tale later. One source told me that the sheriff was attacked by the prisoner and ended up in the hospital. Another claimed that it was tequila, not vodka, and a duck, not an owl OR a goose, and that the whole thing happened inside the Pullman car. One wag said that "duck" was what they did, not what they shot, and that the sheriff was just naturally unconscious anyway. Unkind. We heard the dispatcher caught a cold. But I wouldn't repeat such tales personally. It's beneath me.

I will say that after the Watermelon Seed Spitting Contest, both Wifey and I felt re-connected with the community. And that is important. There's a Chinese auction at the library next week, and *nobody* wants to miss that.

VIBRATIONS

Just one mistake and it would be over. That was the unforgiving world I had gotten myself into down at the County Senior Citizens' Center in the village, and that is why I was racking the balls for a solo practice session on the Center's best pool table. I needed to get better, because the guys I played against were tough and merciless.

I was alone there, racking for Rotation, trying to bone-up enough to preserve my dignity, to be able to stay in the room with the real pool players: to get where I could consistently make the possible shots and maybe get a good "leave" for the next shot. Nothing fancy, just competence. I was tired of the way they smiled when I walked into the room. I chalked up my cue.

But then the rack broke itself and the balls danced away from each other. I felt a trembling in the soles of my feet.

Over at the Ozark Café, Wifey was sitting in a booth across from Old Mr. Hooper discussing the summer's tomato crop, and, as she told me later, a purchase she wanted advice about. He was a veritable font of wisdom in many fields. Then they both noticed vibration rings in their coffee cups—like that water glass in *Jurassic Park*—and then the clatter of café dishes in general, then the rumble outside.

The lazy dogs down by the library yelped and got up off the grassy roadside and headed for safer turf. Down at the Dairy Diner, according to a later account in the local paper, the decorative water wheel actually turned! In the lunch room at the Senior Center, down at the county nursing home, along the benches in the courthouse square, indeed all over town, hearing aids overloaded and had to be switched off or yanked out.

Everybody knew that today would be "different."

We now know that a total of six senior motorcycle clubs hit Greater Jasper for lunch that autumn day. Probably a coincidence. An investigation is now in the works, but the "damage" is done.

***

Probably nobody could have predicted this confluence. Well, an astronomer maybe—someone proficient with tracing orbits of seemingly unrelated celestial objects—maybe. But who can know exactly when or where an errant gang of gray geezers will decide to leap into their leather outfits, mount their pulsing "hogs," and head for the hills for lunch? Who could know that the "Angels" of The First Church of Christ would roar out of Chicago, come down Scenic 7 N and arrive just in time to meet the Bastrop Bug Eaters out of Texas (via 74W) precisely at our little village that day at high noon. And "The Road Hawgs" out of Little Rock? Who knew they would hook up with "The Wayward Wind" out of Oklahoma right where 374 hits Scenic Byway 7 at Mockingbird Hill? "The Okoboji Banditos," a group of very fetching ladies out of Iowa came rumbling in on 74E, and somehow a procession of "Joltin' Jayhawkers" out of Kansas came through Parthenon up 327. All at once? Go figure.

All of us permanent people knew the feeling: the throb, the rumble, the sudden flurry of activity surrounding the arrival of a motorcycle "gang." From the air it must have looked like a bunch of snakes wriggling toward the little town down in the hole, a few dozen hairpin turns away from everything. But we knew the cyclists: we drove with them every day.

Oh, it was not as if Brando and a mob of hellions were invading. We were accustomed to seeing mom & pop teams all decked out in black leather jackets and chaps and ten thousand silver studs, heavy boots, shiny helmets, rugged gloves, various kinds of goggles and face protection—and often tough, tattooed, deliberately photographable characters who looked meaner than some of our own off-road neighbors. And we knew they would dismount, unwrap, and become human. For years, we had heard them, seen them and welcomed them, served them and sold them things. (Sometimes, a community's life blood arrives packaged that way.) Yeah, we knew these people. We just didn't know exactly when to expect them.

***

I put away my pool cue and went to the window in time to see a string of Kawazuki Pathgrinders, I believe. (Or were they Omaha Yamaha Tomahawks? Or RPG's?) Wifey knows more about such things, and she told me that over at the café it was Hondos—led by some huge Drumbuster 1300, or some such thing. I am not good with Japanese names.

For just a minute or two, things looked tenuous. The Harley-Davidson bunch really needs to be kept away from the Kawazuki, Hondo, Yamasheetzu, and Suzaki crowd, under normal circumstances. They disagree on a lot of points. Fortunately, the ones who hit town that day were mellowed out, even some rich guy with a new Sukasuchi Sociopath 3000, with a side car worth more than our home. There was a genuine "Indian" parked over by the bakery, discovered by Old Hooper, who used to ride one in his youth. He took Wifey there and talked her through the details.

All around the square and down the side streets, in neat configurations, I must say, the machines were parked and shut down, and a quiet fell over the town. A great peeling took place everywhere: helmets coming off, zippers and snaps and buckles disengaging, lace and fleece and denim and silk and gray hair boiling out from under leather and space-age alloys and plastics. A goodly amount of eyeballing went on. The locals watched from the Chamber of Commerce storefront, the courthouse, the bank, the little junk shops, and nuts & bolts businesses downtown. And, of course, the Senior Center.

There was a fan-out, and the riders headed for food, some limping a little until they limbered up. Restaurant managers picked up their phones. Hungry senior cyclists jammed the Ozark Café, the Dairy Diner, Sharon Kay's, The Point of View, the Spice O' Life bakery on the square!

Some of the more seasoned veterans of the road, all wearing Harley-Davidson gear, came bouncing into the 'Center and got in line for lunch. They wore jackets, pants, boots, caps, shirts, ties, belts, probably socks and underwear—all branded Harley-Davidson. They were hard core. One very lacy lady—blue hair, chains on her glasses, somewhat bent—squinted through the blinds at the parking lot, obviously annoyed. "Huh," she sneered, poking her husband into looking out the window also, "Jap Crap!" Okay, it was politically incorrect, but the lot was filled with Kawazuki's, and she was a World War II chick. Nothing but a Harley would do for her. About twenty World War II-type bikers hit the Senior Center for lunch, all "Harleyed-out."

I eavesdropped at first, then socialized. The girls in the kitchen struggled to handle the glut. (That went on all over town, everywhere there was food. Off duty waitresses were called in. Relatives had to pitch in. Volunteers stepped up. Someone said Cowboy Jess strapped on an apron over at the Dairy Diner. Old Zeke supposedly offered at Sharon Kay's, but there was no way they could ever explain to a health inspector, so it didn't happen.) The Ozark Cafe went into Saturday Night Mode.

It was crunch time. The town responded. This bunch, after all, had been through the Elk Festival and the Watermelon Seed Spitting Contest, the County Fair, and a Mustang rally or two! They were magnificent.

Motorcyclists cannot explain to normies just what is wrong with a car, why they have to ride out there in the cold and the rain and the snow and the wind and the bugs, or what deep psychological implications are involved in the need for straddling all that power and noise, even in old age. They talk about cubic centimeters and RPMs and cams and things. Baffling. But they don't have to explain to people who know about freedom and beauty and fun and danger. I mingled, understanding that these were the *seasoned* motorcyclists who had probably left miles of skin on miles of road and were not sorry. They were paying their way, and it was okay by me.

The local constabulary and some Highway Patrol and even

National Forest officers slid through town, just as a reminder. Some stopped and looked at one huge, colorful federal-case mill, all black and terrible and towing a coffin-like trailer (equally black and terrible). They gave the impression that we had law and order locally, but that we were friendly. No motorcycle cops were in town, though. They were probably out there zooming through the curves on Highway 7, grinning.

Before long, all around the square, a huge interchange took place, as the foreign and domestic machines and riders mingled. Soon long strings of grandchildren photos were dangling in the middle of small rings of leathery road warriors. Business cards flashed, phone, e-mail, and snail mail addresses went back and forth. There was a great deal of laughter, sometimes cheering and applause, as a group encountered a custom job of great imagination and craftsmanship. Here and there a strange new bike would fascinate a knot of graying adventurers. Cameras were everywhere—digital ones. The bikers nearly cleaned out the post cards, maps, paintings, photography, coffee, spices, jams and jellies, and books, as wonderful gifts and souvenirs to pass on to the family—everything for sale at the Chamber of Commerce shop. I wandered among them, found out who they were, tried to understand. They plundered and paid at all of the shops on the square. They were a merry, clubby bunch.

"I told you: it's the neatest little town in the hills," I heard over and over. And, "All this, tucked away in these mountains—best kept secret in the world." And, "Did you check out that view at Scenic Point? My God!" (God always gets into it.) And, "Greatest ridin' there is. Those curves! Those G's."

I was thinking, "Why do you think they call it Scenic Seven?" But I just relaxed and wandered among them.

All the gas pumps in town were busy with dozens of small sales. If it had been a truck invasion, rather than a motorcycle one, someone would have cleaned up big time.

Wifey was out there taking notes. For a while I thought she was actually going to do an article for the local paper. I lost track of her in the crowd. I thought I saw a tear in Old Hooper's eye as he gazed at that "Indian."

At about 1:15, just off the bank parking lot over by the Revenue Office, the Mayor Himself pulled up on a blue tractor, read a water meter and wrote the figures down on his hand with a ball point pen, then, without missing a stride, gave out certificates to the bikers in an ad hoc ceremony. (That's always important. It brings them back.) A woman from Okoboji had the biggest, heaviest machine, one of the Harley bunch had the loudest one, a little old lady riding with the Oklahoma club had the best chrome, and a couple from Little Rock took the prize for overall presentation (with their magnificent leathers, their Mitzutonka 3200, and their three-room side car). The Harleys got it for Biggest Impact because after they went across the Little Buffalo, it had a head on it three inches high. Computers are wonderful: the certificates looked professional. Some argued later that the blue tractor was unprofessional, but it was what the mayor was driving at the time.

***

By 2:00 they were gone. Not even an oil spot was left behind. These were the old bikers, and old bikers don't leave oil spots. With a final roar, they blew out of town like a summer storm.

***

There was no real crisis, truth be told. The visitors left money, varied the routine, picked up the pace a little, gave us something to look at and talk about—and remember over the long cold winter. There were pictures in the paper, smiles all around. Maybe it all spoiled us a little.

The last time I saw Wifey, she was headed for Buzzard's Roost on a borrowed Sukiyaki 620 (or some such animal) accompanied by her mentor, Rick Roller. Old Hooper advised her to just go ahead and do it. So Wifey's interested in getting a motorcycle now— something that will go when she kicks it. (She likes that.) I've been looking at a Norelco myself, but I think I'm about a year away. If I want the wind in my face, I'll just talk with the pool shooters.

MEANING WELL

Sometimes, despite the nobility of our intentions, our efforts crash and burn. Our mountain is not a place where a "Good Samaritan" gets hit over the head and robbed—not routinely, anyway. There is no rampant ingratitude. People do not take kind gestures for granted. They say "please" and "thank you," and they appreciate kindness. They care about each other, and they try to help out; and people who do help out are the heroes. The value system is sane and solid. But there is something that works against do-gooders, at least part of the time, and makes the impulse to "render aid" a chancy proposition. A pity, I say.

Once, Wifey went over to Mr. Hooper's place to learn some more gardening, and she discovered that a clear glass dish on his table needed to be washed. It was being used for napkins or something. I don't know. I was not going to butt in. He had been "batching" it for years: well into his eighties, a widower. But Wifey put the thing in his dishwasher for him, and the machine did its job, washing the object very thoroughly. And then we got a phone call: Hooper couldn't find the glass thing because it was clean and clear and he could no longer see it. Go figure. Spent half a morning searching for it. Wifey meant well.

Then one day Wifey had trouble on the mountain. Her tiny toy car—an Australian built Ford product—blew a hose about half-way down to the village. I was at home, minding my own business, and I got a phone call. "Your wife's car broke down a coupla curves up from the fair grounds. Best get down there." It was someone local moving down mountain and carrying a cell phone. She called me so that I could be the hero, I guess. (In the city, a stall could draw obscene gestures, curses, even gunfire.)

So I leaped into my pathetic pickup and headed down Scenic Seven. It was only four miles, but when I got there I could not get near my wife's car. Good Samaritans from four states were on the scene, and the highway shoulders were jammed with cars, and traffic slowed to a crawl. A big RV from Mississippi was sitting there, and I found Wifey inside having coffee with a nice lady from Tunica County. They were talking about stained glass. Her quaint little car was being worked on by a cluster of men, all arguing about the strange engine, whose hose would work best (there were several), and whose coolant would replace that which was lost. They didn't want to talk to me.

I had grown accustomed to this type of thing in the years since my retirement from the city, but I must admit that this was a bit much. The coffee-in-the-RV thing really got me. She was my wife, and I thought it would be politically correct if I went on record as having helped at least a little. (Save more trouble further down the road—my road!) These folks told me that I was not needed and that everything was under control. They offered me coffee, and they didn't have any Diet Coke—but offered to go into town and get some. Someone offered *me* a blanket. And it was early September.

It took law enforcement officers from three agencies to break up the party. But the whole thing taught me that this impulse to do good was epidemic!

***

Sometimes I was the primary target of the kindness. I was "Done Unto," as some say. When it was determined (behind my back) that I should bowl, my friend John (not Annie's John—Bowler John) gave me a bowling ball of my own. He just got it out of a flower bed at his home one day, as if it had grown there, and he gave it to me, complete with a carrying case. An act of friendship: a man helping a fellow man. We shined it up, and it was a good-looking bowling ball. But there I was, now, with a bowling ball of my own—just as if I could actually bowl or something. I felt like a blind man with a sniper rifle. I eventually procured my own bowling shoes, too, and I would waltz in there and stake out an area and put on my bowling shoes and unzip my spiffy bowling bag, and yank forth my shiny personal bowling ball and pose there, all smug. And then I would step out there and bowl a 103 or worse.

It seemed unfair to me that, although I was a good person, a kind person, a degreed person, and an AARP member to boot, I could not bowl worth squat. Little old ladies would set their crutches aside, limp up to the line, dump off the ball, and lay waste to the pins, trouncing me. An old man with one prosthetic leg and a hook for a hand buried me—routinely—week after week. A granny who *looked* like a bowling ball handed me my head! Wifey beat me by 20 pins. John offered me another ball. John's wife blamed the shoes. They were all kind, except Wifey. And I could not quit because of that wonderful gesture of friendship: I owned my own bowling ball and shoes. I bowl regularly now, to the amusement of all, and I just know I'm getting a bowling shirt for Christmas. God knows what it'll have printed on it. I am sure everyone has good intentions.

***

Food is an area of difficulty in these parts when you're talking about meaning well, having good intentions, helping your fellowman.

During tomato season, everybody has tomatoes, even those who can't grow them. Those who can grow them spread them all over the hills, until everyone has bushels of them, and more tomatoes become a threat and a burden. But nobody refuses fresh tomatoes, because nobody wants to offend those who can grow them (next year looms), and nobody likes waste. And everybody likes tomatoes. A lot of canning gets done.

It's that way with a lot of things when the crops are ready for harvest. According to Old Hooper, if it's yellow squash that you've got, though, the thing to do is put them all in a big bag, sneak up on somebody's porch, set down the bag, and run like hell. It's worse with zucchini. And turnips. Green beans come by the large brown grocery bag, and once they get going they won't relent. Pumpkins are largely ornamental, but you can end up with several metric tons of them if you're not careful. And early in the summer, bales of leaf lettuce and spinach—fiber and iron enough to stuff everybody. All those acts of kindness can blow right up in your face.

You almost invariably elect to give corn-on-the-cob to toothless folks, and you rush over with a big apple pie for the closet diabetic just over the hill, and you have a peck of potatoes for the couple trying the Atkins Diet. Tiny mistakes. You have to be careful. Any overdose of anything can cause trouble.

Wifey frequently offers my chili when some group is going to have some sort of picnic or supper. They serve chili dogs and make a little money. But my chili will barely freeze! It is volatile chili, best measured with a seismograph outfit—best served under medical supervision—best kept away from children and Senior Citizens. But nobody will refuse my chili, because I am proud of it, and nobody wants to hurt Wifey's husband. I have watched them work at these affairs, and they mix my chili with wimp chili donated by someone else who never lived in Texas, in a pathetic attempt to dilute it. I know their tricks, and I zip in a little extra *Blazin' Saddle,* just to kick it up a notch. And I like the way the fumes rise and dissolve the paint on the ceiling. But people should be careful with my chili.

One of the ladies about six ridges west of us creates the most hideous concoction imaginable and dashes over to every mourning family with it, proud and beaming, "all smiles" at the funeral. The creation is arguably a casserole, and it contains both animal and vegetable matter (of this planet, most agree), but it becomes an unidentifiable, solid puddle of disgusting, indigestible muck at her hands. Nobody will tell her about it, because it is her specialty, her baby, her pride and joy. She collects "Thank You" notes, and that is as it should be, for ingratitude doesn't work in the hills.

There is another lady who "sings" at the slightest provocation. Apparently nothing can stop her. If you have fillings and have chomped down on some aluminum foil, you know the pain caused by the sound of her voice. Nobody will tell her about her caterwauling because she does it for free and can therefore be accused of no real statute crime. When she crosses over in a few years, they'll send her to The Tuner first, I predict, and then St. Peter—and *then* she'll get her harp and take her place among the angels. She means well.

***

Out of "the goodness of my heart," I gave one of my wife's girlfriends a subscription to a magazine one Christmas. She ended up getting mail from a hundred charities, clubs, societies, organizations, institutes, and magazines. Same thing happened when I entered someone's name in a contest at the state fair. Go figure. Instead of winning the DR Trimmer, he started hearing from gardening people from Guam to Nova Scotia. I just wanted to help out. (That junk mail is good for starting a fire on a frosty morning, though. We manage as we can.)

I bought chances on a camouflaged 12 ga. shotgun from a nice young man at the county fair—benefiting a worthy cause, I am sure. Now the NRA "would appreciate my support," and I am being watched by the FBI and the game warden. And I already have a shotgun of my own. The boy is blameless, and I should have won, of course—but no hard feelings. The boy was doing his best, and I was just "taking my shot."

***

One day I told a lady down at the 'Center that her hair looked nice. (How was I to know it was a wig?) Wifey nearly took my leg off with a well-aimed kick powered by the training she was getting in the 'Center's exercise classes—which I had encouraged, and, I suppose, subsidized. When I tried to retract the statement, she got me in the other leg. I shut up, and she jumped me for being sullen. Go figure.

So the next morning I said to Wifey, "My, you look good today, Dear."

And she said, "What do you mean TODAY? What was wrong with yesterday?" I heard about it all day long. She can look as good as she wants now, but I am "snake bit," as they say in the hills, and I shall not comment.

***

And sometimes well-meaning "folks" create tragedy. A few of the "girls" decided to help out a lady they knew whose house had gotten a little past it. It was messy and dirty, and the lady was not feeling very well—so the ladies (the church bunch) decided to make a raid and help out. And they swept in and swept the place out, cleaned it up, washed it down, took care of the bathrooms and the bedrooms and the linens and the laundry—even gave the lady herself sort of a make-over. Some of the men came over and fixed up her yard. Nicest thing I've ever seen done. I was proud of all of them. Then that lady's daughter came in from the city—back East somewhere—and put her mother into the local nursing home: said she apparently couldn't take care of herself anymore. There was a For Sale sign in the yard ten minutes after that little hussy hit town. Probably went away with a Power of Attorney, too.

The church bunch visits the lady regularly now, at "the home."

***

One miserable winter day Granny Benthurst was being rescued, and just naturally resented it. She lived alone out in the county well off the end of the tether, and all services to her place were cut off (downed lines, terrible roads, etc.), and it was only through a miracle and a great deal of determination that EMT's and other rescue, National Forest, Park Service, Fish & Game, and law enforcement people were able to get to her—out there all alone in a very iffy house, with the mercury dropping and the skies looking even more ominous than before. She was being rescued, but nobody had asked her about it beforehand, and she was not amused.

"What are you people doing on my land?" she scolded, leveling a shotgun at the intruders. "You better git!"

"We just want to know if you're all right, Ma'am," said an EMT.

"You're trespassin'!" Granny yelled.

A Fish & Game officer slipped around to the side as the EMT tried to work with Granny.

"Don't you want to come into town where it's warm? We don't want anything bad to happen to you."

"Just git!" And she tossed a round over their heads. A distant vehicle got sprinkled with some #8 shot. "Somethin' bad could happen to *you*!"

"Well, are you warm here? Do you have food? Are you safe? Does your phone work?" There was a wood pile, a little chimney smoke, signs of life, but still…

"Son, that's none of yer business! Now hit the road!" And she let fly the other barrel. The rescue squad left, giggling a little, and Granny went back into the house and shut the door.

Later, it was decided in a 5-6 vote, that Granny Benthurst was a wait-and-see situation. But the Fish & Game officer's input was influential. He had noticed that Granny had a field-dressed deer hanging on her back porch, and he surmised, from a hole in her screen door and blood by a fence out back (around the little family graveyard), that the old gal had nailed the animal with probably a 30/30 right from the comfort of her kitchen. Granny had just been toying with them with the shotgun, and she probably did not need rescuing just yet. Maybe next winter. Maybe not.

Some of that got into the paper. But, according to Old Zeke, the deer was deemed a legal kill (an emergency situation), and Granny did send a "Thank You Anyway" note to the sheriff. Those boys meant well.

***

In fact, many instances of random or impulsive acts of kindness have been documented in this region. A local arsonist had to set his house afire three times before he managed to make an ash of it— because the neighbors kept putting it out. (An insurance technicality understood locally.) A young man in the area supposedly ran into a raging house fire and rescued a litter of kittens. They were unwanted and unnecessary kittens until that story broke, and then they were precious little miracle babies, set for life. Another of my friends nursed his lady friend through her final days, a coma, her death bed struggles, the moment itself. Her family, who had been absent throughout, came out of the woodwork (some nasty urban place, no doubt) and raised a stink about their "improper relationship" there at the end. Alas, they were not married. Good intentions all the way by one and all, probably.

***

In the Buffalo River Valley and in areas around the valley, the park service started an elk herd. Seed stock were imported and released. There's a little stone monument about it on the side of a hill. A wild river, and wild elk. What could be better!

And the elk had few enemies, and they went forth, and they multiplied. Today there are herds of elk running around, eating the farmers' crops and potentially spreading diseases to the deer and the cattle of the area. They are handsome critters, too—especially their little blond butts. And there's no turning back now: they are a significant part of the local economy. Hunters come from everywhere and spend, well, for want of a better term, big bucks. The money is needed, and the elk live here now. The elk is on the town logo, and there's a festival about it. It's a done deal.

To make a "national" river out of the Buffalo River, hundreds of people (including veterans who had placed their lives on the line for their country) were forced (by their country) out of their family homesteads. We The People gave them a choice: this will be a lake or the best natural canoe river in the country. The property owners moved out of their slice of Paradise, but the river is saved forever, for the good of all.

To stay alive and feed their families, many local men cut trees down and saw them up and haul them away in very inconvenient logging trucks—block traffic—damage highways—make "tree huggers" furious—but feed their families and send their kids to college, and punch up the local economy. People will actually come into the hills from the cities to fight on behalf of those trees— meaning well, also. But, of course, "Those aren't trees, mister, they're tuition for my kids' college education."

Hey, silver linings would be a bore without the clouds. The silver linings are pretty, but the clouds bring the rain. It's all about point-of-view.

***

Because we are "called," not merely "drawn," to acts of beneficence or solicitude, we cannot pout when they go awry. We cannot simply quit—shut off the thoughtfulness, the philanthropy, or the noble desire to do the right thing—just because of a little trouble. We can't go away and brood in the woods about it. (We're already in the woods.) We have to go on with it, collectively and individually. Apparently, it is about impulse, not choice, and we are stuck with it. Evidently, we will always come running—with the fire hose, the casserole, the bumper jack, the hot cup of coffee, the blanket, the gesture—whatever it takes—to rescue, salvage, comfort, repair, or somehow save the day. Out in the hills, that hasn't been torn out of us yet.

And if there is anything I can do for you, let me know.

THE WASTELAND

Every morning, as I told all of my city-pent friends, I could step to my window, sip on my wake-up Diet Coke, and witness beauty such as one might expect of Heaven: variety without fail, mystery, intrigue, drama, challenge, unfathomable spectacle. Daily. As a matter of routine. That was what we bought into, and that was what we had—even on stormy days.

Details of the landscape changed little, day-to-day, but the seasons worked their magic, the clouds were dependably whimsical, and light played games moment-to-moment. A pond, a rock, a distant peak, a tree line, a road or trail, or an ant-like vehicle on the move could be a surprise anytime. I could never get enough.

Then one morning in about our third year, I gazed out the window in the prescribed manner and nearly screamed. "My God! Look at what they've done down there!"

"What?" said Wifey, moving over to the window.

"Down there—to the right—near 374. To the left of that tiny barn." And I pointed and handed Wifey the binoculars and guided her to the horror.

"My God! They cut down the trees!"

"A wasteland. The idiots have installed a wasteland! It was something we didn't have, so they went down there and put one in! Great. Just great."

It was true. There was now a huge scar on the land where there had been forest before. How had they done it so fast? We had not seen one tree go down—not one bulldozer scraping things away—not one scoop picking up rocks and piling them up on the edge of the horrid defilement! We had not seen logging trucks, brush hogs, skidders, nothing! There was even a pile of smoldering debris, and we had not seen the main fire! We felt violated.

"Does this mean they can take all of the trees if they want to? Why don't you call up somebody and put a stop to this?" Wifey snarled at me.

"But...but..."

"Get on that phone and call the sheriff. Call the state police. Call a lawyer. Why don't you go down there and stop them!"

"It's five miles away..."

"So drive. Don't just stand there! You just let people run over you."

"But..."

"You have no force. You hate confrontation! You're gonna let these people just rape the landscape."

"Well, I..."

"Never mind!" And Wifey got on the phone herself and spent the rest of the morning learning the horrible truth: It was a valley, it belonged to people, it was not mere scenery, it was not under our control, no crime was being committed, we had no say in the matter, it was part of living here, it was not there for us alone. We could just as well learn to enjoy it.

I lifted my eyes and looked at the rest of the landscape, and it was still wonderful. It was just one patch of bare canvas in the giant landscape masterpiece. But Wifey looked at me and sneered in disappointment. Again.

***

Friends from the city eventually found us and dropped by on the way to Branson and points North. We had told them about The View as best we could, and now it was time to get them out of their car, drag them around back, and present the spectacle, and watch and listen as they were overwhelmed.

I must confess that I was a little embarrassed. I hoped they could forgive the terrible scar on the land—the abomination, the sacrilege. But I did not try to guide their eyes.

"Oh," said the lady, almost immediately, "look at the beautiful meadow!"

"Meadow? What meadow?" I asked.

And she was looking at and pointing to my wasteland! Out of the whole view, she had picked out a patch of clear-cutting, and she liked it. It was now full of lush green grass, and a few Herefords were grazing there. For her, it was the focal point of the landscape. It was as if the works of man were part of Nature to this woman. Go figure.

"That used to be trees," I told her.

"Oh. But it's special now!"

"Special!"

"Yes! It points to the beauty of the remaining trees. But it has individuality."

"Oh. You could be right. I don't know." I looked to Wifey for comment, but she just shrugged.

"It was part of the forest before, but now it's a place unto itself," the lady said.

"Okay. We can live with that. I suppose."

***

I guess that wasteland is a meadow if she says it is. Everybody runs over me. I guess it's special. Indeed, when I think about what we actually look at out our window, I suppose we are drawn to the interruptions, the points of contrast, the marks of man and math— roads and buildings and fences, and meadows—blended into the natural scene. Maybe my wasteland is actually beautiful—and not wasted at all. Sometimes it's hard to tell the canvas from the painting.

DANCIN' IN THE KITCHEN

When you're married—really married—there is a danger that you might settle for just staying home on Friday night. When you're a "Senior Citizen" suddenly, it is worse. (And you do become a Senior Citizen all too suddenly.) Then someone comes up with a ruse to get you out of the house one Friday night, and you jump up and go, if you don't want to "miss out."

Wifey and I were eventually drawn into a little circle of zealots who gathered on Friday nights down in the village to appreciate a certain strain of country music. A small band rented the City Hall annex and held sort of an open rehearsal, and they played and sang the Saturday night songs—the sad songs, so sad they became funny—the "somebody-done-somebody-wrong" songs—the painful, empty, lonesome songs about tired lovers giving up, giving in, or giving out. We knew all about the struggles, the conflicts, the "heartaches," and the honky-tonk despair sequence where all you have left is a worn-out car, an empty bed, and a cold cup of coffee—when, as the saying goes, it comes down to "a bottle in front of me or a frontal lobotomy." Like so many in the room, we had been there and done that and were over that, mostly.

We were there, on a tip from Old Hooper, our aging garden buddy, for the fellowship and the food (Old Hooper's specialties). Just off the relatively small main room where the band set up its P.A. system and a scattering of metal chairs, there was a kitchen with an "island" and a fridge and a micro and plenty of countertop. You could do a chippy-dippy-punchy-cookie hit, or you could get into sandwiches and coffee and cakes and pies, often decadent and sinful. All pot-luck, too. You could contribute some nummies from home, or you could toss a little money into the kitty for the rent of the hall, or both.

"My God," Old Hooper would whisper as he shuffled into the kitchen. "Ain't it wonderful?" And he would join the grazing. It was a line he used while harvesting his tomatoes and sweet corn. "Ain't it just wonderful!"

The mandatory steel guitar cried out in pain, the electronic drummer kept the beat, a bass guitar and a rhythm guitar joined the lead guitar for the instrumental stuff, and two "girls" pitched in, singing the high notes and harmonies and all that. They usually had song books laid out before them. It was indeed a rehearsal, and the group tried new ways of doing the songs, sometimes stumbling, missing a beat, laughing, starting over, trying again, and ironing out the problems. It was a warm-up for Saturday night. Meanwhile, about thirty people would have a great evening, and life would go on, just like in the songs.

And the sadness of some of the songs literally became a joke. The skinny old boy on the steel guitar would slide in an agonized sigh at the end of a heart-rending phrase, and the teardrops would fall, and the band would laugh—laugh because of the melodrama or because of the perfection, or maybe because of whatever it is that gives people the giggles after a funeral has gone on for a while. There was a "sadder than thou" attitude: "Watch this. I can make this song sadder." The musicians would "milk it."

***

Friday night, for lonely people, has only one thing going for it: it is not Saturday night. You don't have to do anything on Friday night when you are alone—you can rest. You have an excuse. It has been a long week. It is the night before Saturday night. But if you don't have anywhere to go on Saturday night, or anybody to go with, that is brutal, and it is the makings of a country song. "Hello, walls..." and "I'm so lonesome I could cry..." "The last word in lonesome is me." When you have lived such nights, that does not seem like exaggeration. This was a rehearsal for the brutality of Saturday night.

Wifey and I came to enjoy the sessions. I was skeptical at first because of the language difficulties. Old English teachers do suffer so. But then, "Why not?" we would agree, "It's a gig, and TV is terrible."

***

The band hit a streak of divorce songs that one Friday night—put a few of them together back-to-back to test the effect, I suppose. They spelled it out: D-I-V-O-R-C-E as the actual lyrics to a song. I could tell that many in the room had known that pain.

Wifey and I were "veterans," too. We had picked each other up off the ground years before and were now like two sides of a step ladder, leaning. The divorce songs hurt. Divorce hurts. Like most groups, those around us that night sported some gray hair, a few lines and wrinkles, some tell-tale postures. As the painful notes were played, pairs made contact—touched or smiled or nodded—something. And we belonged.

"Put your sweet lips a little closer to the phone..." the song goes, "and pretend that we're together all alone..." (Yeah, they're separated.) Everybody knew that one. And when the band got into that song, "He'll Have to Go," I was feeling gloomy myself, even though I was in the kitchen with Wifey and some Diet Coke and a ham & cheese and some rippled chips.

There was something happening around us, though. The audience was involved in the song, but not attentive to the band. I looked around and followed the focus, and I saw. Two people right in the room with us were totally involved, and burning down.

"Of course," I mumbled.

Everybody knew everybody—and everybody's business and everybody's story. The ruined politician, a handsome man with freshly darkened hair (we knew) stood transfixed in one corner of the kitchen holding a cold cup of coffee and an empty paper plate. Across the little room—across the "island" table groaning with pot luck food and drink—a lady with a new dress (we knew) stood with her own cold cup of coffee and paper plate. And, for the two of them, the world went away—just like in one of those songs.

We all saw it. It was that old "across the crowded room" thing from Rodgers and Hammerstein. It was like Tony and Maria in *West Side Story*—but with vintage people, all grown up and almost old (we knew). Better yet, it was Old Tex spotting a veteran Saturday night gal across a dance floor in a dive in West Texas. Her marriage had crashed and burned, and she had been "waitressing" and housecleaning and treading water for years. His marriage had exploded while he was in office at the state level, and his career was now toast. Both had been in a thousand country songs in the void following divorce. All of the platitudes applied (we knew).

And now they looked at each other and saw each other for the first time, and the music was terrible—sweet and yearning and full of all the suffering they had known. (We remembered.) It was as if the reason for all of those songs had been revealed.

There's a bumper sticker that says, "Lead, Follow, or Get Out of the Way." Everybody decided to just get out of the way, first just there in the kitchen, but then it spread to the main room, even to the band itself. The ruined politician put down his cold coffee cup and his empty paper plate and moved over to the lady. And then they were dancing, right there in the kitchen, by the refrigerator— dancing a slow dance, gazing into each other's eyes, past the damage, slowly melting. Then they were just swaying and holding on. Then they were just holding on.

The doorway to the main room filled with faces, then the opening leading to the office areas, then the serving window between the kitchen and the main room. Sandwiches dangled half-eaten near mouths that needed to smile. Paper cups half-lifted, were fondled like crystal wine glasses. All gestures were given up, withdrawn. The harsh fluorescent lights seemed to soften to a romantic 3 a.m. glow.

The lead singer fell into it right away and began to improvise words like,

"On a Friday night in autumn
As the band began to play
I looked up and saw two people

Who had come a long, long way.
And they caught each other lookin'
And they liked the look they seen,
And they reached out to each other
Over everything between...

Or something like that. It was smoother that night, less grammatical. You had to be there. But like the swaying couple, the singer was making it up as he went along.

They were dancin' in the kitchen,
And their troubles went away.
They were swayin' to the music
From a sadder, darker day...

Well! The steel guitar picked up right where it was needed, sobbed out the improvised tune as if it had been written long ago. The girl singers joined in: "They were dancin' in the kitchen, and their troubles went away..." And the couple by the fridge held on, eyes shut, drifting.

There was one of those awkward moments then—when the curious catch each other peeping or eavesdropping—and they feel like cruel voyeurs. Then everybody pulled away, the way good people do when they happen upon a sleeping innocent. We tip-toed away and let them have the moment. And the kitchen. The music went instrumental. No more words were needed, but silence would have been shattering. Only guitars would do now—or maybe violins.

It wasn't going to be one of those small town gossip pageants you hear about, either. There was something spiritual going on, and everyone understood. The dancing pair reminded us of old wounds, of healing, of lost opportunities, and of scars of our own, and of "last chance" rescues. These two had hit refuge after a terrible storm. The Friday night gang "got it," and those who stayed home that night missed out.

***

When Friday night was over, we said our good-byes to our friends and stepped out into the cold, crisp autumn air to head up our dark mountain. And you know, I took a good look at Wifey, and she looked, as Old Hooper put it, "Mighty good!" And I went up the mountain that night feeling like a lucky, younger man.

FELIX DALBY, SCULPTOR

When inanimate objects "misbehave," I believe they must be punished, preferably by those whom they victimize. My mother always credited *things* with attitude, will and personality, and she was right. I insist. I know that they act alone, and I believe that they conspire *together* against us when necessary.

As an old English teacher, I admire rhetoric. When a chain saw refuses to start, when a tire willfully keeps losing air, when a stone reaches up and tries to clobber my sore toe, I believe in Language! Those things need to be called what they are, in no uncertain terms. When a coffee table reaches out and barks my shin, before I kick it, I hurl a volley of expletives worthy of my education. When a hammer gratuitously hits my thumb, I classify and categorize that hammer with ghetto-inspired invective and then throw said hammer out into the woods. The hammer knows what it has done wrong as it flies into the brush, and I feel better.

I have received an education that only junior high and high school teachers understand. In the hallways and classrooms, and the restrooms and lunchrooms of the public school, I have learned from our children language that makes me ashamed of my human form—that makes my skin crawl—that nauseates me and disgusts me. When I am one-on-one with a willful, vicious object, I fire away! And I was so innocent once. Pity.

My computer has been called every foul name known to modern English, and a few from antiquity, plus a few Arabic unmentionables I have picked up. This is a quiet, back-room procedure, of course, nothing fit for polite company. I keep all of this strictly between those objects and me. Other humans get mere sarcasm. If it is wrong, God will get me for it.

But it should be no surprise that I not only understood, but also admired and respected the deed that was done down in The View, near the Log Hall, under Red Rock.

***

Felix Dalby was in the throes of a divorce. More of a war, actually. Divorce gets that way sometimes. Felix had become a victim of the local economy, and his wife of several years had noticed it, and then mentioned it, and then obsessed over it, and the blessed union had crashed. Lawyers got into it, and decisions were made. Sad, messy, very public.

Well, it would not rain, after all, and so there was no river—no canoes, no "floating," no business. And Felix was in the canoe rental/ river-running business, like so many locals. It was seasonal, and when you lost the season, you lost your butt. The economy of the household could not take it—not again. No money, plenty of bills, lots of fights. Kaboom.

Oh, Felix could have gone to a "chicken outfit" and packed or cut up or even killed chickens, or hauled them around. His wife told him that several times. "Go gut chickens." Fact was, though, that he knew no Spanish and couldn't "cut it" in the chicken/produce industry, which was now flooded with newcomers from Mexico.

Besides, how could he work inside after the river? How could he give up the clean-flowing water, the cliffs, the sky, the sun, the mountains of his daily life? It could rain any day. Floaters could flock in from everywhere, anytime, and give him at least a modest, last-minute rescue. He had to be there.

The courts, however, spoke. Felix got half of the canoes, half of the guns, half of the house, half of the equipment (trailers, etc.), and half of the Jeep. There were no children.

The court awarded his wife the old Chevy (worthless, but transportation), and half of the Jeep, which was worth more and was in better condition. They never said which half.

Among the equipment that Felix "won" in the fray was a large chain saw, and one night right after the gavel fell, he walked through the house and lopped off half of it. The lady promptly had that half picked up and carted into town, leaving the rest for Felix, out there under Red Rock. It was all in the paper at the time, with photographs of the sliced up house. They were a zany pair.

But Felix continued to drive the Jeep back and forth to menial jobs he was able to pick up in the area (some kind of wrinkle in the divorce papers, I suppose). He would do anything to stay—to hang on until there was rain: water, tourists, floaters, salvation—anything to save his way of life. I couldn't fault that.

We had him up to the house to do some heavy digging and chain saw work. That's how I know about the deed that he did— down there below Red Rock.

***

We worked together half a day out back. I noticed that Felix believed as I did: stubborn and rebellious tools and lids and doors and rocks and logs needed to be, well, *cussed* a little, just to explain who was boss. Blows needed to be struck, and colorful expressions needed to be flung about. We worked well together, making sure to plug the ears of the innocent, warn The Lord, and, as Felix said, "Keep the women folk up to the house." (He was as polite and civilized around the ladies as I.)

I did have to ask, though, while we were working out there and dealing with stubborn things. "Did you ever hit your wife?" And he said no, and that she had brothers, and that there was a code. He took off his greasy baseball cap and put it over his heart when he said the part about the code. I understood.

Later, after we had finished the work and I had paid Felix and he was supposed to be gone, he knocked on the front door.

"Have you got a screwdriver I could borrow?" Felix asked me.

"Phillips or flat?"

"Well, both. Damn carburetor gives me fits. It needs to be done unto." And I could see that he had that Jeep peeled down in the driveway, looking forlorn. And I know Felix knew what he was doing under the hood of a car because he had an STP t-shirt on—either that or he got it at the same place I got mine (a thrift shop), cheap, but functional.

I saw there in the driveway the way the Jeep was treating him, and I would testify in court if asked. It would cough, then start up, then when he slammed down the hood, it would just quit. Vicious. He would open it up, tinker with the carburetor some more, get it started again, and softly lower the hood, then carefully climb aboard, and then it would quit and sit there and smile at him. Then it would let him get all the way to shifting it into reverse, and it would shut down and sit there looking innocent. Nasty. It was provocative behavior, I am prepared to insist.

Felix was eventually able to get the beast running, and he returned the tools and left our neighborhood. I thought the thing staggered a bit as it went by the little church a few hundred feet down the road. Gravity would get him most of the way to what was left of his home if the Jeep balked again. I stood and looked down the road after him with great awe and admiration.

It was a miracle, you see, that he got the thing out of our driveway. And I must say that, for a common man, Felix was able to regale that stubborn machine with some exceptional rhetoric. In fact, I expected the paint to peel right off that one side of the vehicle. He reached way back into the hills—deep into the "hollers" and gulches—down into some nasty slough holes in the nether regions of our language, and hawked up some really tacky terminology. I was impressed—and in full agreement. Almost nauseated. But that Jeep deserved what it got.

The next time I saw Felix, he had "done unto" that Jeep.

***

Sooner or later, I was bound to run into him again, I knew, but I did not push it. It was a small county, and you kept seeing the same core people over and over. Half of the cars on Scenic Seven honked as they went by, and we found that we more than likely knew the person stopped at the stop sign at almost any intersection—or in the next booth at the café, or in the next aisle at the grocery store. I would run into Felix sometime.

So when Wifey and I were at the fair grounds entering my poetry and her jams and jellies for judgment, I was not surprised to encounter Felix Dalby one more time. What surprised me was that he looked so much better—so much more at peace—even self-satisfied—"together" and resolute. The harried look of the man who fought his Jeep in our driveway was gone. He had gone from t-shirt and jeans to sun glasses, pony tail, Greek peasant shirt, cargo pants, and bandana.

"So, what brings you to the fair grounds, Felix? Peaches? Pickles? Wood carving? Quilting?"

"No, I'm sort of a sculptor now," he said with a grin.

I tried to imagine a statue to his ex-wife, created with the love and affection spawned by the divorce, rendered in elk dung, and run through by a spear. (Our county is big on elk.)

"I did not know you were a sculptor. I had you for a man of words. I want to see this sculpture."

"You will. What did you enter?"

"Words. A poem," I said, "a poem about gardening and revenge. Wifey has entered jams and jellies."

Felix nodded, gave me a thumbs up, and drifted off his way, and we went on with the processing. Time passed, and on the day when the awards and ribbons were passed out, Wifey and I contritely entered the appropriate building at the fair grounds, hoping our efforts were winners. I had little hope for my poem because I had chosen to use blank verse, and blank verse does not rhyme. I had confidence in Wifey, though. I had been into some of that good jelly. I was not thinking about Felix.

But the stir, the hubbub, the disturbance, really, at the county fair was not about jam or jelly or produce, not poultry or poetry. Not even goats or llamas. It was about art. It was about sculpture!

The bullet-riddled carcass of Felix Dalby's Jeep was sitting inside a ring of frenzied people in the middle of the floor in the judging area, draped in ribbons. *Grand Champion! Best of Show! Special Artist Award! Most Original Creation!* All of the awards I wanted for my poem or Wifey's jam. Felix had shot his Jeep.

"Well, you saw," Felix told me later. "She wouldn't behave. I called her everything I could lay my tongue to, and it didn't do no good. So I started on the Old Ex's half of the thing—shot out her headlights. Once I had her blinded, she was helpless. Used a 243, a 357 magnum, and a 12 gauge, then finished with the .22. I woulda used the 44 magnum, but *she* got that in the divorce—for her purse gun."

Indeed, every part of the Jeep was full of holes—bullet holes. All of the windows were gone, all lights were shattered, the tires were flat. It looked like Bonnie and Clyde's car at the end of the movie. It looked like something from Downtown Baghdad. Even the personalized license plate with his former warmer's name on it was perforated. "Marge," I think, but chewed up a lot.

It was justice, I say. And it affected people—evoked a response, so I guess it was art. Maybe he had to give his Ex half of the ribbons. I never knew. But I am sure that I have noticed other Jeeps in the county running very smoothly, taking care of business, and behaving. The word is out. (Jeeps communicate with each other, you know.)

And Felix Dalby has an avocation now. His card says, "Felix Dalby, Sculptor. Canoe Rentals and Custom Metal Sculpture."

Anything to stay in the hills.

***

One lady at the fair thought it was tasteless to call the shot-up jeep art, but Wifey pointed out that her friend Lacy, a fair volunteer, got a Reserve Grand Champion ribbon for her sack lunch, purely by accident—ended up getting a check for $2, enough for a hot lunch at the Senior Center. Who is to say?

FUN DAY, FUN PEOPLE

E verybody asked where you were," Wifey said, "and I didn't
know what to tell them."

"I was whacking weeds in the back yard."

"But it was Fun Day at the 'Center. You promised that you
would be there."

"No, I said I would probably be there. But then I got involved
with whacking weeds. My blood was up. I was laying waste to those
rotten weeds! Then I looked at my watch, and it was almost lunch
time. I came right down."

"You missed everything. Old Zeke took off his shirt and threw
it in the air—all of the men did. People laughed their heads off. It
was the wet T-Shirt contest. He looked white, like a cutworm."

"A wonderful moment..."

"HE is a fun man. The plumber had the Best Chest—
officially!—but he couldn't get the girdle past his hips."

"Girdle!"

"HE is a fun man. Looks bad in lipstick, but HE is a FUN
man. And that one pool player—he's tall and skinny, has a white
and bloodless look, gangly legs and arms. HE is a fun man."

"Yeah, I've always said that. He's such a great pool player. I
respect him."

"Old Hobson looks terrible in mascara, and he can't wear a
dress. But HE is a fun man. And that other pool buddy of yours—
the one from Oklahoma: he's got great legs, but he has a belly, and
he thought the girdle was for one leg. But HE is a FUN man."

"Sounds like he is."

"And the love handles! When they all got wet and turned their backs to us so that we could see their calves and their backs, you should have seen the love handles! I laughed until I cried."

"Flab everywhere, huh?"

"And knobby knees! THOSE men are the fun men. All that rouge and lipstick, the girdles and bras, the kick line..."

"Kick line?"

"Sure—a kick line! It was a spectacle."

"I respected those men once. Their powers of concentration, their precision..."

"We laughed until we cried. They were good sports. You whacked weeds."

"What really humiliating things did the women do?" I asked innocently.

"Whaaat?"

"I mean, what completely debased, degrading, mortifying things did the women do?"

"Decorated hats."

"No wet T-Shirts? No girdles? No taking off their shirts? No flab shows? No varicose vein displays?"

"We decorated hats—got a prize for the best hat."

"I don't suppose anybody lathered up and shaved or put on a jock strap or jockey shorts or anything."

"We decorated hats, I told you. We wore ridiculous hats. But those men who got out there and made complete and utter fools of themselves, THEY are the FUN men. YOU whacked weeds."

"Yep. Sounds like I really missed something. Women all over the hills could be talking to their husbands about my love handles and sallow skin and knobby knees."

"Next year, you're in the show."

"Yes, Dear. Next year. I can hardly wait, actually. I will be the joke of the county. It will be devastating, absolutely crippling. I may never recover. Next year. I will be fun."

A lot can happen in a year. Me? I'm gonna fertilize those weeds and pray for rain.

LIKE A TOURIST

The car in front of me had all of the tell-tale signs. The license plate was produced by criminals of another state, the speed of the vehicle was about 25 mph., except on the sharp curves when it got down to 10, arms and pointing fingers were bristling from the windows, and there was drift at certain points—over the center line or dangerously close to the shoulder. Tourists on board.

It was a daily fact of life: some tourist would get out there on Scenic Highway Seven and attempt to make my trip to town a real journey. If I missed the lone opportunity to pass, just a couple of curves below Scenic Point, I would have to rot there at the wheel all the way into town. If it was a logging truck, the driver would pull over at a spot designed for that kindness; if it was a load of chicken entrails that was somehow not flipping over and dumping its load that day, it, too, would pull over. But a tourist was oblivious. And that day I had me a tourist, right in front of me.

I gripped the wheel, my knuckles turned white, I gritted my teeth, and I got ready to cut loose with a colorful barrage of language especially designed for these annoying occasions. I had a little imaginary button on my steering wheel that I could push and shoot out an imaginary rocket that would explode under the tourist's left rear wheel and dump him over the side into the canyon. I also spent energy imagining a system whereby we locals could plug into the tourist vehicles and make them a deal: pay them to get off the road and out of our way! Then we could go on with our important trips to Bob's Market or the Post Office or the Senior Citizens' Center or... Never mind.

But that day, something odd came over me like a tiny fever. I was screaming, "Who do you think you are?" when I suddenly wondered who it really *was* there in the car in front of me—and what he was going through. And then I felt foolish. How short my memory was!

I glimpsed left and right, and the familiar things were there—the very things that brought Wifey and me to the mountains in the first place. The valley was a bowl of feathery white clouds that morning, and here and there those clouds would reach up over the highway. The sun was shining down on all of it, and we (my tourist and I) could see from above—but then we were descending, getting under the cloud layer, into mist, then overcast, changing densities, changing colors. A doe and two fawns were feeding on one shoulder of the highway. Red bud trees and dogwood trees were in blossom, and a number of wild flowers were crowding the road. Then we popped into sunlight again, and off to the right we could see all the way to Missouri. An eagle checked in, right on cue.

Both my tourist and I drifted over the center line and back over to the shoulder, came to our senses, held on to the wheel and tapped the brakes. I could almost hear the people in the other car, with their oooos and aaahhhhs and other expressions of wonder. Soon, for them, I was shouting, "Look at that! Just look! We're up where we belong! We could almost hang a right and drive right off into the sky. If it gets any prettier, it might explode! Take a picture, somebody! Take a picture."

And I learned to pretend I was one of them, seeing it all for the first time. I was riding the brakes again, hanging on for dear life: thrilled and terrified and overwhelmed. At the same time, I was yelling to them: "Check out the cliff! No, on the other side! That's all ice in winter! That's Missouri way out there—thirty-six folds away. How about that bamboo! Here's where you climb Round Top. Don't miss this stuff! Don't miss anything. Sharp curves ahead."

It was good for the soul—and the blood pressure. And for me it was a new way to get into town. It's how I drive the mountain these days: slow and easy, fully involved and full of wonder, like a tourist. One of my friends does it that way, too, and claims that all

the cars are piled up behind him because he is a magnificent leader!
Works for me.

Art by Scott Baldassari.

BEYOND ELVIS

It was a day when the Ozark Café, downtown there, on the square, was being the Ozark Café of story and legend with all of its might. It was being what Double-Dog Darrell (resident wild man) idealized, dreamed, and fantasized about, and what Justin Kase, local poet laureate, had written about: a coffee house/meeting hall/revolutionary headquarters for the newly lost generation, and a window on the world.

It was miserable outside—cold and damp and blustery—very autumnal. The leaves were already down and mostly cleaned up around the square, and the bib-overall bunch on the bench over by the courthouse had a session going despite the cold. That was the other meeting.

In the café, Double-Dog Darrell, Cowboy Jess, Justin Kase, and I were having the *important* meeting around the big table with Rick Roller, a relative newcomer—a hyperactive fire-plug of a man who had been running amok over the back roads and river bottoms of the county for several months as if he had to absorb it all by Christmas and go away—or die—or take off for Mars—or wherever he came from. The guy wore us out just telling us about his systematic, fine-tooth combing of the area. (He was my candidate for Poster Boy for Adult Onset Attention Deficit Hyperactivity Disorder.) But he was calm if you didn't provoke him, and he had met with this bunch before. There was coffee and Diet Coke and potential at the table.

A tourist entered the café with his wife. Tourists could just as well have banners around their necks labeling themselves. Same with married couples. We found out later, after it was over, that they were from The Valley—the Rio Grande Valley of Texas—up our way having a look at the colorful leaves (and visiting an aunt in Mountain Home). They took a booth quite near our group and began looking at the treasure-trove of historical photos that decorated the cafe.

"Well, there are a lot of things we can't control," said Cowboy Jess, as if we had been talking about control issues for hours.

"Yeah," said Double-Dog, quickly adjusting his eye patch, which had been up under his slouch hat earlier. "They have wars, spend our money, jerk us around. Nothin' we can do. Except get mad and kill everybody."

He said the last part rather loudly, and the couple in the booth pricked up their ears. I could tell that they were settling in for some quality eavesdropping. I couldn't blame them, really. We were settling in, too.

Cowboy Jess had his ten gallon hat on (for he had been a real cowboy in his heyday), Justin Kase was wearing his windblown New England poet outfit (complete with incredibly long scarf), and Double-Dog was fully weirded out in tourist-baiting regalia. I looked like a retired English teacher that day, as usual. And Rick had been riding his motorcycle and looked like a piece of bad road. He was muddy and weather-beaten. We looked interesting, if I do say so myself. We had been sitting and gripping our caffeine in silence before. But now...!

"Settle down, Double-Dog," I said, putting a hand on Darrell's arm. "We can't kill everybody. It would be bad for business." He growled like a large animal, and I soothed him and lightly restrained him.

"Hey guys," said Rick, "I saw a place this morning that I bet you've never seen."

Well, Double-Dog and Cowboy Jess had been everywhere in the county at one time or another, and I knew that remark would get flak, and color up the conversation. I checked, and the tourists were tuned in.

"It would have to be a new place," said Cowboy Jess, and he sipped on his coffee and looked off into space—not right at anybody—like he saw smoke signals on the horizon or something. (As he said, he had "some Injun" in him).

"Oh, it is," said Rick. "You may have been there before, but it's all different now. Most people would be surprised at who's livin' out there in those woods." He laid that last sentence right out there for those tourists, in sort of a stage whisper.

"Speak," said the poet. "Enlighten us. Trip our triggers. Fire our imaginations, and give our fears wings." He whipped out a notebook and a pen. (I thought that was a bit much, really.)

"Well, you know where Grundy's Notch is?" said Rick.

"Sure," I said for all.

"Well, you go West of there, and you hit a road off to the left—pretty good road at first. But then it gets bad." Rick smiled right there, relishing the memory of the terrible trail.

"That out there by the Moon Cult in them bent-up double-wides?" asked Cowboy Jess.

"Way past them. Further back in there, past where those hippies and hermits live among those rocks."

"Friends of mine," said Double-Dog. "Used to ride together—back before the accident."

I sneaked a peak at the Texas folks at that point, but nobody else did. The tourists started leaning in. It was wonderful.

"Oh, yeah—the accident," said Cowboy Jess. "Bad scene."

I hadn't heard about any accident, but I knew it was meant to be a hanging thread—just an artful thing Jess had thought of—so I did not ask the question.

"Sounds like that's the road that goes up there by that counterfeiter's place—the guy that lives in the Saran Wrap house," I offered.

"That was me," said Double-Dog. "I lived in the Saran Wrap house. They burnt me out. Get your stories straight."

"Sorry."

"No, it's past the counterfeiter, and it's past that compound where the old pedophile priests are living while they're waiting for the Statute of Limitations to kick in."

"Oh, I heard about them: I just had no idea where they were." I thought my role here was to stimulate the real conversationalists.

"No sign of life there, though. Of course, I could still motor at that point. But then the road files off to a point and turns into more of a trail, right by that old de-programmed CIA guy's dug-out." Rick turned on that little grin of his.

"Bet yer gonna talk about that fella in the Witness Protection program," said Double-Dog. "Tell us new things, or I'll rip out your throat and feed it to the hogs." And he growled again. I soothed him.

"Easy, Double-Dog. Behave," I said. Darrell was adding a little spice, going for the edge of madness routine. I calmed him.

"Naw, it's past the Witness Protection guy. Way out—past the Chinese nudists—past Old Zeke—even past the hillbillies."

"The real hillbillies?" All of us registered amazement here. Good form.

"Yeah. Off the end of everything."

"You're talkin' Way Out," said Justin Kase. "You're not supposed to go out there. Nobody is."

"Nobody does," said Rick. "But I went." He had a glow about him. He had really been there—or somewhere interesting.

"Past Elvis' place?" asked Double-Dog, raising one eyebrow.

"Shhh!" came from everybody at once, and all of us looked around for hidden mikes, eavesdroppers, spies, snitches, something! It was gettin' good!

"Yeah," said Rick, "beyond Elvis." And he looked around nervously, eyes just huge. "With the leaves down, a sort of path develops. The leaves are wet, and they lay still, and you can see a path. So I went on. Real quiet."

"Was Jimmy home?" asked Cowboy Jess. And we all looked around again, very guardedly, I thought.

"Hoffa? Sure. I know he was there, but he won't talk to nobody, and you can't see him. But it was past Hoffa's place."

"I keep telling' yuh, that ain't Jimmy Hoffa. He lives out by Ben Hur, with Miss Amelia—in that buried school bus," protested

Double-Dog Darrell, hissing and snarling. I tried to subdue him. "The guy you're talkin' about was a Project Blue Book guy."

We were all hoping the tourists would pick up on Amelia Earhart. Certainly "Miss Amelia" was enough, right? I noticed that their food was getting cold, and they were doing more listening than eating. Delicious.

"You better be careful," said the poet. "There are strange things done out where you're talkin' about."

"I went beyond Elvis," bragged Rick, "beyond the last still, past Bigfoot's lean-to, across Satan's Slough, past Black OP Billy's tepee, downhill from the Watergate burglar, and then uphill—out there in the wilderness, past that hut where that Manson cult member lives, and the cave where that clown from The Grassy Knoll is buried."

"It's called the Grave in the Cave," said the poet laureate. He was writing in his notebook again. "And you better leave Black OP Billy strictly alone."

"Well, I went on past all that, until I had to get off the bike and walk."

"You *were* out there," I said. "I've seen you ride."

Then everybody went silent for a full minute. The poet was scribbling furiously, and each of us posed and made sure the tourists were paying attention. The waitress had been slipping in and out, quietly taking the order of the Texas folks, getting their drinks, etc. The two of them were silent, too, but attentive.

"Well, did you see Mad Sheila?" asked Cowboy Jess. And I know nobody had heard of Mad Sheila. But Jess made her up right there, and we had to take her and run with her.

"Naw. I saw some hair ripped out by a blackberry bush, and a little blood, but not Sheila herself. Something mighta been chasing her. There were some peculiar tracks." Rick was really good at this.

"Sheila will be all right," said Double-Dog. "Maybe she was doin' the chasin'. She hunts alone—with her bare hands. And she does leave some peculiar tracks." Darrell was good at it, too.

Silence again. We decided to just let it ferment for a while. The tourists stirred their cups vigorously and eyed each other. The poet started waving his pen to a beat that he had been working with on paper. Then he held his book out at arm's length and adjusted his glasses, and tossed his long scarf over his shoulder. It was possible to imagine a cruel wind on his face. The rest of us focused on him.

"Beyond the King of Rock and Roll,
And past the guy from the Grassy Knoll—
And down the trail from the CIA
And the burglar guy from Watergate—
And the peacenik/beatnik/surf bum shack,
And the Black OP creep who still ain't back..."

He stopped there because that was all he had down on paper, but he seemed pleased with his work so far. "I'll call it *Beyond Elvis*," he said, and went back to work.

Finally, "There's a mansion out there," blurted Rick suddenly.

"You lie," said Double-Dog, as if charging Rick with murder.

"I never lie," said Rick. "You go out there past that cave grave, up the rocky ladder, then make that last dozen feet straight up in that rock chimney, and when you pop out, there's a mansion!"

"Good Lord," I gasped. "How did it get there?"

"There are no tour guides," said Rick, fondling his vanilla Diet Coke. "Nobody to ask. But it's like it just got beamed down. It doesn't belong there—know what I mean?"

We put in another silence sequence here. It was uncanny how it all was agreed to, just with a little eye contact. We had to let it all sink in.

I had heard about big construction projects, modern homes, wealthy or dangerous seasonal or occasional tenants, all very hush-hush. The electrical people know all about such things. The mansion part was real. I insist.

"Well?" said Justin Kase, lowering his pen.

"Well what?" said Rick.

"Did you get in there and find out anything?"

Rick grinned. "You know I did," he said smugly. "I always go in there and find out. And you'll never guess who lives there."

"Osama?"

"Anastasia?"

"Clinton?"

Everybody guessed, rapid fire.

"It's a spooky place even in daylight. It's big, and I'll bet it's worth a million five. Not here, of course, because you can't get to it. But it's there, it's a good 8,000 square feet, and it's got everything. And I had to know who built it, how it was built, and what the hell it's doing out there in that wilderness. So I just went up and knocked on the door."

"You don't mean it," I said, glancing at the tourists.

"Just went up and knocked on the door," Rick repeated. "It was an old door on a new house—looked weather-beaten, like it had been on a lot of mansions for a thousand years. Big white pillars all around, lots of dark windows with moving curtains! The door itself looked haunted. It had a knocker—a big brass door knocker with a twisted face on it. I knocked anyway."

"Well?" said the poet impatiently.

"Well what?" said Rick.

"Well, who answered the door?"

The tourists leaned in closer, not breathing.

Everybody looked straight at Rick, and there was silent agreement: the exercise was about over. Just a couple more touches.

"I've knocked on a lot of doors in my day, but..."

"Who answered the door!" thundered Cowboy Jess for all of us.

Rick stood up dramatically, extended an arm, and pointed. "HIM!" he shouted, pointing at the eavesdropping tourist in the booth.

Double-Dog snarled wildly and tried to spring, but I physically restrained him. Justin Kase did a beautiful spit take, knocked off his hat, and dropped his notebook, in one fluid motion! Cowboy Jess reached for his six guns, which were not there anymore, of course. We were magnificent.

The tourist guy recoiled like he had been shot, and his wife screamed and upset her water glass. Then there was silence.

Realization. And then, of course, we all just howled—waitress, cook, tourists, we tasteless fools, everyone! Soon introductions were in order, all around, and some arm pumping, apologies and some back slapping. We all chipped in and bought the couple's lunch.

***

Yeah. It was all a little game we played. Tourists, you see, like to think something strange is going on in these hills, and sometimes we play with them. I once heard about someone who used to growl and scream in a cavern just below a scenic overlook—for the tourists! Hey, it gets turgid in small towns sometimes. You make it up as you go along. It keeps us sharp. The tourists want to believe, and we help. Tourist baiting is a fine art. It was ending together, the way we did that time, that was wonderful. We were like those jazz players, and the bluegrass boys: we all ended together after the chaos of creativity. It was a great moment.

***

I resolved to get Rick to take me out there, though—out there beyond Elvis—if I could ever get him to admit that the mansion part was real. I know it's real. I am ready for it to be real. A mansion, way out there. I like it. All Rick does is give me that little smile.

BLIND FOG

It was stupid of me. Wifey let me know that at the time, and she was right. Again. Somehow, I got involved in something useless in town, and when I gathered my senses about me, it was dark outside. Okay, I was gambling. Just shoot me. I was down there at the Legion Hall playing Bingo with Rocko and the bunch, and overdosing on trail mix (the accepted snack), and Wifey was stuck at home because she had a batch of bread baking and couldn't get away.

Wifey hated to be alone on the mountain at night, and so did I. And if there was one thing nobody wanted, it was to be on the road after dark in a blind fog. It was October, and fog was not unusual. I left the Bingo game and headed up the mountain, hoping for the best. At that point, I had little choice.

At about the fairgrounds, a few sharp curves and a few hundred vertical feet up from the valley floor where the town is, things got misty. As I slid up along the base of Round Top, things got murky. I hit the low beams, and continued slowly, but I knew where this was going. I was inside a big, wet, dense, cold cloud, and I couldn't see anything in front of the car. Things got opaque.

We usually roll down our driver-side window and use the center line as a guide in such instances, but the state boys had been working on the road that day—a little re-surfacing and punching up the shoulders, getting ready for winter. And there was no line. The line would be painted tomorrow, or next year, and, no doubt, a bunch of us would smear it all over the road before it dried. But all I could see now was black: brand new asphalt—two or three feet left or right or...never mind. I was in trouble, and totally disoriented.

If I stopped, someone could come along and smash into me—

from behind or ahead, it made no difference. If I continued, I could smack into a cliff or go off one, depending on which side of the road I found. I could luck out and find that I was near a pull-out, and get off the road, and just sit there until the cloud blew away. Or someone else could blast into me on the pull-out. Or, not.

I felt my way along, once hitting rough stuff on the right and veering to the left a little. I tried "feeling" the right shoulder with my front wheel, but that soon failed. I tried remembering from the hundreds of trips I had made up that mountain.

A lot of people around here admit to praying at such times, and those who say they don't are liars. I slowed down again and again, and then just stopped. I thought that if I could just get a look at the surface of the road—walk around a little, maybe, I could at least figure which way to move the car. But it was a choking fog, thicker than I thought possible, and every ray of light just formed a wall. Against all of my instincts, I opened the door and stepped out.

"Lord," I said, "You could move this cloud and let me get home. No big deal. I promise I'll never play Bingo again."

"You can make a better deal than that," a loud voice said—from three feet away, right in front of me.

I screamed, of course—a manly scream, but a scream for sure—and I jumped in the air like I did the first time I heard a rattlesnake. The other fellow screamed, too. And a horse neighed right behind him, and then a cold nose touched the back of my hand, and I leaped again.

"Double-Dog, I swear to God…"

"No you don't. I heard you. You were trying to cut a deal. You want to give up Bingo in return for safe passage home. And you were very polite."

Double-Dog Darrell was out there in the fog. Maybe he was part of the fog, I was never sure. (Once he told me he was the wind.) But he had his dogs with him and his horse, and we were all in a pull-out, safe and sound. Oh, I was on the wrong side of the highway—had crossed over the other lane and gone off the road. Blind fog, Blind luck. I had picked berries a few feet from that very spot just last summer. I had stopped just short of a plunge into the woods, downhill.

"What are you doing out here at night?" I charged Darrell. I could see that he was all geared up for a ride, foul weather anticipated. He had a camouflaged slicker over everything—not that I would have actually seen him. He was invisible. He was the wind.

"Night is the best time. I keep tellin' yuh that. How many lessons do you need?"

"I just need to get home."

"This'll blow off. It's movin' around fast tonight. Want some trail mix?"

Double-Dog, eccentric or not, was a comfort to me. I felt almost safe. His wolves all said hello in their way, and traffic was not a problem. There was none. We had a short meeting in the glow of my headlights, and, as I was promised by Double-Dog, the cloud blew away in a few minutes—temporarily. It is amazing how the mood changes when the fog blows away. As an educator I should have remembered that. Or maybe shared madness is comforting.

"When you think about it," DDD said pointedly, "we all run around in a fog most of the time. Of course, sometimes the details just get in the way." And he grinned, and I knew I was supposed to go home and stay awake half the night pondering those words. I was more likely apt to spend time trying to find value in them.

I went on my way, and DDD went on across the highway, I believe, perhaps for an ascent of Round Top. Yeah: at night, in the fog. Why not? Someone must. I'm still working on that.

There was a heavy mist at Mockingbird Hill, and a pocket of thick stuff on the curve just before Gum Springs Road, but by then I had a center line, all the way home—quarter of a mile, I'd say.

COWBOY AND INDIAN

Sometimes in the dead of night I felt the woods pressing in on our little outpost on the mountain, especially at first. A brainstorm or indigestion or guilt or remorse might have me out of bed and staring—pacing and probing—and I would feel all of it out there together, like a living being.

Then I would cut it up into manageable lots, and work with it, and play with it. As a high school English teacher, I was trained in handling the overwhelming, after all.

And that is when I happened upon the phenomenon of Cowboy Jess and the image of him out there somewhere on a lonely bluff burying his horse. I had tucked the tidbit safely away one morning a year or so before, but there it was one night, and I had to deal with it. I still have little 3 a.m. episodes.

***

He was a real cowboy in his day, Jess was. Oh, he was part Indian, but all cowboy. He rode the range on a horse, he broke broncos, he herded and branded cattle, he tangled with rustlers and rattlers and lonesome coyotes, and he toted a gun (probably an old .44). He also did the rodeo circuit—a world of trailers and trucks, bulldogging and bareback bull and bronco busting brutality, miles and miles of road, Marlboros, women, and whiskey. It wore me out just hearing about all of it, first hand or through others around the county who knew him.

I met Cowboy Jess on my front porch when he showed up one day in our first year on the mountain and offered to help me paint the front porch the wrong color (Shutter Green) if I would have the missus rustle up some grub—or something colorful like that. We painted, we talked, and Wifey got together a decent lunch, and we got through the day.

After that, whenever I saw Cowboy Jess, it was "on the fly"—he moving in his orbits and I in mine. I noticed each time that I encountered him that he was becoming more and more civilized and I was becoming more and more "countrified." He was getting out of denim and leather and into cotton and polyester, and I was going the other way. Down at the café the day I found out about burying the horse he had on his Stetson and I had a sweatshirt from the high school where I taught for so long, but both of us were now in bib overalls. Common ground.

"What color is the porch now?"

"Brown. A dirty brown."

Sometimes it was more of a red, and for a while I had it stripped and it was just a woody-looking mess. Cowboy Jess was just opening a conversation that could lead anywhere—maybe to serious stuff: career stuff.

"What made you drop out of the world?" he asked me.

"Burn-out," I said, "and opportunity. The same folks who wanted to work me to death left open the door to escape, and it all worked out. How about you?"

"Old age—and, of course, my horse died." Right away like that—up front in the conversation.

I could understand the old age thing, even though I was not quite there yet. But Jess reminded me of Richard Farnsworth in one of those Western movies about an aging cowpoke nearing his end: *Death of a Salesman* on horseback. He owned virtually nothing, he was a mental wreck, and every bit of his life was embossed on his body and his face. Old cowboys end up drinking coffee in a café somewhere, and looking like seven miles of bad road.

But a dead horse into the bargain? I had to ask.

"Yeah. Old Stony had been with me for a lot of miles. We hitchhiked through the American West, you know."

"You *and* the horse?"

"Yup. I'd stick out a thumb and Stony'd be right there beside me pawing the ground, and we'd get picked up by a big rig—at a truck stop or a pull-out or a rodeo—and we'd go on down the road."

"You don't see a lot of that," I ventured. I was thinking about a horse on the roadside thumbing away—but with a hoof. Never mind.

"Yes you do, really—it's out there, but it's not a world a lot of people know about. We wouldn't try for a Volkswagen or a Mercedes, you know. But we could get picked up by a stock trucker. Got around good—for years. But then, when all that was over, out here on the mountain a few years back, Old Stony just couldn't make it anymore. Died on me, right in the middle of July, 1987. That about did it for me."

"Rodeo horse?"

"Sure. We did it all, me and that horse."

I could imagine the parts I had seen in movies or at rodeos, but nothing Cowboy Jess could say to me could make me understand what his horse had been to him. I knew about cutting horses, and I knew about the ones that got the bulldoggers and ropers to the animals. I knew nothing, really.

And in the night, later, all I could visualize was a man, a pick and shovel, and a dead horse, somewhere out there on a beautiful mountain in summer. The seeds of the image were planted down in the village at the café, and then, in the night, like some of the meals at the café, it returned to haunt me.

"It takes a big hole to bury a horse," he told me, "and the ground around here, especially high up..."

"I know. Believe me, I know. If you want soil up there, you haul it up there."

"And your shovel says 'clank' right away, the second you hit the ground with it. It's pick work, and lots of back! And I wasn't feelin' very chipper, either. I loved that horse."

"I thought they went to rendering plants—after. I mean I thought they went to glue factories or..."

"Not family. When a horse is your brother, it rates a grave.

Old Stony's got a grave and a stone, and I don't know where they get glue."

"Good for you, Jess."

"Yeah, but it was a heap o' diggin'—if I can put it in plain terms."

"Go ahead. I'm not teaching English anymore."

"I dug and scratched at that hill for hours and hours. I suppose I could have gone and got a back-hoe, you know—or a dozer. Any number of old boys around here coulda done for that horse in nothin' flat. But I figgered I had to bury my own horse, you see what I mean?"

"Absolutely." I thought of dogs and cats I had already put into the woods near our house, animals that had won me in an instant, made me care, then stepped out on Highway Seven.

"We had been through Texas, Oklahoma, New Mexico, Arizona, Utah, Nevada, Wyoming, Montana, Colorado, California, Nebraska, the Dakotas, Missouri—you understand?"

"I do. I think so."

"It's special with a horse. I don't suppose you ever knew a horse personally. You're what's called a 'come-here.' From the city. I'm what they call a 'come-back'—I was born right out in Boxley Canyon, growed up, hit the road, got into a war or two. Worked at the King Ranch in Texas, then did some rodeo. Then I came back mostly. Picked up with that horse in Arizona, and we did a lot of miles together."

"Good thing you owned some land here."

"I never owned no land."

"But the grave..."

"Well, there was trouble, because the horse ain't buried on any land of mine. It's government land these days, and it was then, too. And some yard bird heard about what I did out there and wanted me out there to dig Stony out of the ground and move him."

"My God. I knew they evicted veterans from inherited family land, but..."

"Oh, they didn't evict no dead horses. The government won't mess with sacred Indian burial grounds."

"Oh, it was an *Indian* burial ground?"

"Well, it is now. I knew a few braves from Oklahoma—Cherokees—shirt-tail relatives. And us Indians got together some papers, made some claims, and threatened all of them government boys with an embarrassing pow-wow of protest. And nobody wanted any part of sorting out the bones—of deer and buffalo and Indians and horses. There are other bones out there, too—from other things. Got us a real treaty! I could take you out there sometime—if you don't mind a few ghosts."

"Indian ghosts?"

"If you say so. Anyway, Old Stony's out there on his mountain and in his grave, and it's real purty out there. Indians understand about horses—and men—and ghosts. Sometimes governments forget."

***

So, I'm up in the night now and then thinking about Old Stony—haunted, I suppose. Cowboy Jess is fading fast these days, and he will probably never be able to take me out to that mountain. He wants to be cremated and scattered out there by that horse (when the time is right), but he won't tell anybody around here exactly where it is. Someone over in Ardmore has all the information. One of those Cherokees. I haven't made any promises or plans, and I hate to think about it, but when the time comes, I think I would feel privileged to be out there when Old Stony and Cowboy Jess get back together.

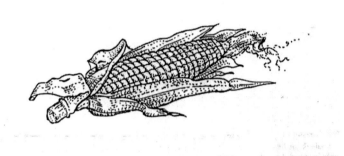

THE DAY OF THE CORN

"Next summer, I'm gonna show you-uns how to eat corn on the cob, right out of the garden," Old Hooper promised Wifey and me, "and it's gonna change your lives."

It was November, just barely November, and we were starting a dinner that would happen in July of the following year. When you think about it, all meals start that way—far before the act. We had just walked the garden spot, but we were in the house now, out of the cold wind.

"We'll get us some Silver Queen. To my mind, that's the Cadillac of sweet corns. Kandy Corn is great, and Peaches & Cream is good, but you-uns are virgins when it comes to eatin' fresh corn on the cob—right out of the garden and straight to your lips—and I'm gonna take you on the journey, and it's got to be Silver Queen."

"Silver Queen it is," said Wifey. Me, I'll roll over for just about anything that is food.

Old Hooper started his garden "ten minutes after Christmas," if he could wait. But he was "pumped" about this one, and we were responsible. When we met him, he was 86, almost 87 years old, and he was talking about hanging up his hoe, parking his tiller, and turning himself in at the nursing home. Still, he was running all over the hills with bags and baskets of fresh garden produce for anyone who needed it or wanted it, and that is how we found him. He had a lot to teach, and we had a lot to learn about gardening, and I was always hungry. We inspired each other.

"I've had corn on the cob all my life," I said. I had spent a lot of time in the city, but I was a small town kid from way back, and I had lived in Iowa and Nebraska.

"You ain't had Silver Queen right out of the garden. Nothin' eats as good. Little butter, salt and pepper—tomaters—cucumbers—all ten minutes from the vines! And I'm gonna spin a chicken out here on the rotisserie outfit, and we'll set in the shade and watch it go and listen to the little motor and wait for it all to get done."

Then he paused and had a shaky sip of coffee. "Haven't done that since my wife died on me," he said, and his eyes glanced toward the mantel over his fireplace. We had studied the picture of her before.

"Then I'll show you how to cook it a special way. Then we'll get it on the table and slather it with butter, and salt and pepper it, and we'll jist wash our ears with it!" I could almost see that cob of corn at his mouth, like a big yellow harmonica, back and forth, and the image of washing our ears hit home.

"Sounds like a plan," I said, looking at my watch, and I started waiting right then.

Wifey likes to take care of people. Old Hooper did not need to give up and head for the nursing home, as far as she was concerned, so she stepped in and helped with some of the logistical things. She had been a nurse in the front lines in Houston, so she knew how to talk to agencies and pharmacies and the people who run them. She knew about how veterans and Senior Citizens in general get shut out, passed over, and notified with gibberish in six point type. She knew about callousness, and she could get past it.

Also, as her personal Sherpa, I can report that she can usually point what is left of my musculature in the right direction. I would be helping where I was needed.

We became a team, and the journey to the perfect meal shoved off. I began smacking my lips when Old Hooper picked up a pencil and showed us how he would start—ten minutes after Christmas—to lay out the coming garden on paper. I was ready to go out and buy the butter right then, but Wifey reeled me in. Hooper's old trembling hands drew a rectangle on an unlined piece of paper, and I was ready to eat sweet corn.

"The tomater plants will be about seven feet tall," Old Hooper told us on New Years Day. "We'll get the post hole digger and set the stakes—eight foot poles out of the woods."

I had seen tomatoes grow before, but seven-foot stakes seemed exorbitant, and talking about them in January seemed premature. Old Hooper had, upon occasion, been forced to prove to strangers that tomatoes grow that tall, and that things growing that tall were actually tomatoes.

"Nothin' better with corn on the cob than a plate o' tomaters. Super Steaks! Run about two pounds apiece." He was steadier now. Wifey had phone-whipped some medication, and the stuff was beating his tremors.

"I like a smaller tomato," said Wifey.

"We'll grow you some, then. But when we have the corn, we'll eat the big ones!" And he had that glow about him, and I made another feint in the direction of the butter. Down, Boy.

By February, Wifey and Hooper had the whole garden planned: the lettuce, the spinach, the corn, the tomatoes, the radishes, the little green onions and the bigger ones, the cucumbers, some kohlrabi, carrots, strawberries, watermelon, cantaloupe, turnips, squash, potatoes, collard greens, beets, garlic, sweet potatoes, a few English peas, and some experimental, ornamental, ridiculous beans and peas. Everything was planned. Hooper was one of the finest educators I had ever met.

"It'll all be good, but the big day is gonna be tomaters and corn on the cob. And I'm gonna make a cobbler."

"I'll get the ice cream," I said. "Blue Bell—out of Texas!" I began waiting hard—with slammed-shut eyes, straining!

"It's February," Wifey reminded us. "We haven't even got the seeds."

"We'll all go to Springfield," said Hooper.

And we did, too—went out of state and got all the seeds. Hooper bought $50 worth! Wifey laid in a supply for our own humble patch. We put together a whole day trip revolving around the coming garden season, and the upcoming dinner.

Our lunch in Springfield went practically unnoticed. "Butter, salt and pepper—and sweet corn. You haven't lived yet, but the day's comin' when you set down to my table. Chicken, corn, tomaters—it don't get no better than that."

"Diet Coke," I offered.

"Sody if'n you want it. Me, I gotta have my coffee."

"It's only March, guys," said Wifey. Then she mentioned something about chocolate. Wifey was waiting hard, too.

We ate other meals together, at our place, and "out," and each meal was an occasion to talk about and anticipate THE meal. We went through the corn, kernel by kernel, cob by cob. We savored those tomatoes and cucumbers. Hooper walked us through the chicken, the salt, the pepper and the process of wrapping the cobs of fresh corn in wet paper towels and micro-waving them. I could almost hear the climactic DING announcing that the corn was fully zapped and ready. (Wifey had advocated boiling a vat of water, like ordinary folks with ordinary corn, rather than micro waving. This was, however, not your ordinary occasion.)

If there happened to be a crop failure, it would be a complete disaster for all of us. We were set up for it. The Day of the Corn became a fantasy, then a dream, then an obsession. Through the plowing and the planting sessions, I became convinced that no meal of any kind could live up to Old Hooper's anticipation. We sat out under his shade trees and talked about everything else, and then about THE dinner, bite by bite.

"I'm gonna get the rotisserie out, just like I did when my wife was alive, and we'll knock the rust off and start it up for a dry run. We can jist set here a while and run the motor and think about that chicken—them tomaters—and all that corn on the cob."

We were not eager to sit and listen to the labored whine of the rotisserie motor, but we made the scene for Old Hooper. "Used to set here with my wife and spin a big old chicken—sometimes a roast—every other Saturday night in summer." And we listened to the little motor, and I could see Old Hooper drifting—drifting back to other times. He sipped coffee with a steady hand and looked at the empty, spinning skewer. It was a look you see around camp fires. We quit talking.

Wifey and I learned a lot, and the tomatoes, despite complications, did climb up there nearly eight feet. We planted corn three times before it was over, and all of it did well. We tilled, we fertilized, we hauled water, we pulled weeds, we talked weather until we were worn out. And the garden grew.

In early summer the Mother Lode came in: everything right on schedule, more of every crop than all of us and the whole Senior Center mob could eat. Hooper was zooming around the hills with produce for everyone—all free—for the assisted living apartment folks, the shut-ins, the lonely, organized food agencies, passers-by, favorite waitresses, Wifey and me. It was his hobby, his joy, his identity, his life. And he was deeply happy. "Ain't it wonderful," he chirped. "Ain't it just wonderful. It's all a miracle, every year!"

***

So, the big day—The Day of the Corn—arrived. It was the middle of July, and my wait (our wait) was over. I contributed the ice cream, and Wifey found some Amish butter that was a cut above. I wanted the sweet corn, but I wanted the ritual more. Wifey was ready, too. And Hooper floated around on a cloud of golden mist! We met, reverently, at Hooper's place, just before noon. It was time.

***

I don't know the answer to the obvious question. It could have been ashes, I suppose. It could have been mediocre—or magnificent! But, by the time we got to that meal, it was certainly magic. Maybe it was really as good as we just knew it would be. But when you do anything with someone who takes such immense pleasure in doing it, the enjoyment enfolds you. As we "washed our ears" in that corn on the cob, we knew that there was nowhere else on earth any of us would rather be: that this moment was the "be all and end all," and that it represented something unforgettable that all of us needed. We did all of this for each other. We were a little family, in an off-beat, beat-up sort of way. We had put together something akin to love. And nothing else mattered.

SAVING THE OLD BARN

I have passed the old barn over a thousand times. It is right there on the way to town—another of the sights that challenge my imagination and my ability to mind my own business—right there in daily life. The temptation is always there to hop over the fence and trot out there into that field and have a look inside.

I can imagine ghosts of goats and cattle, horses, barn owls, feral cats, mice, snakes, perhaps mules, and people. The place has to be full of rusty old hooks where hand tools once hung, worn and wooden pegs where harnesses awaited their moment—maybe the faint smell of ancient manure, the dust of old straw. It would be dark inside, and there would be shafts of sunlight slashing in, highlighting forgotten spots on the dirt floor. I can almost hear the milking going on: the rhythmic pulses of the sprays of milk, first with that metallic, bottom-of-the-pail sound, then the lower sound as the milk puddles up, then gets deeper in the bucket—and an interruption or two for the occasional treat for the alert cats, waiting. I can feel the warmth of the moment, being there next to the warm cattle, the contentment, the fulfillment. There had to be children, too, and hard-working people, the flutter of doves or pigeons high up in the rafters. I know about such things. I didn't spent all of my life in the city.

But for a reason I cannot identify, I have never visited the old barn—penetrated it, explored inside. We just keep driving on past. Someone put a wonderful metal roof on the barn a year or two ago, and I was glad, because it meant that someone cared about it and would not let it simply die. Long ago, I had seen barns die, in Minnesota, during my whole childhood: a lonely structure, leaning more and more with each season of neglect, weakening and hanging on like anything dying of age, and then, unseen, settling into a forlorn heap. I was happy for this barn, under its new roof, but still I did not go there.

Naturally, I tried to analyze that. Old English teachers like to read a lot of meaning into things. Was there some subconscious terror, some dread memory, some sublimated phobia? Had I been a milkmaid in a previous life? An owl? A barn swallow? I came up with nothing, and decided that the old barn evidentally did not matter to me. Well, not enough to pull off the road and just do it!

***

Then one day I was dragged off into a cave. The hills are honeycombed with caves, apparently. I had been inside the managed caves, and I had been just inside a wild cave or two, and I had learned enough so that I had no desire to go where I was not necessary—to ruin some eco system I had nothing against. I did not care about stalagmites and stalactites, and I had no desire to snap any off and bring them home. Nor did I want to carve my name or leave oil from my fingertips or otherwise sully some innocent cave. But one has social responsibilities, so I've been on a few cave trips. (I guess you can't call them "outings.")

Somewhere, there is a photograph of that day's gang inside the cave. I look fat in it. We went to the legendary Lost Valley (a location everybody alive has found), and we penetrated the cave—reputed to be a hole straight through the mountain and out into the aforementioned "lost" valley. It turned out that the lost valley was the one we had just hiked through getting to the cave entrance, and that the cave led deep into the mountain, a cul-de-sac, and that, if you wanted to see daylight again, you turned around there and re-traced your route. It was cool inside, and everybody enjoyed the trip. A stranger took our picture.

But I noticed something. I had been at the mouth of that cave before, and I had not gone inside. Wifey and I had decided to save it for a later date, and we had spent our time enjoying finding the lost valley and *speculating* on what was in the cave. After all, it could have been a hide-out or fortress for an outlaw gang or a band of rebels. Everywhere else was. There might have been a treasure in the cave—from Spanish days, perhaps. (Lord knows the Spanish couldn't manage their gold: the floor of the ocean, the beds of the Mississippi and the Arkansas Rivers, the Gulf of Mexico, the Carribbean, the Atlantic Ocean, and any number of islands are weighted down with Spanish gold—just littered with it. Ask anyone, read anything. They couldn't get it home to save their souls. The deserts and mountains of the Southwest, too—gold everywhere, from those hapless Spaniards. And the Confederates were forever losing scads of gold, too. There are books and books, maps and maps.) So this cave could have been wonderful. The *speculation* was the important thing.

Alas, it turned out to be just a nice cool cave. We crawled in there, stood up, huddled together, got the picture, and sang, "Amazing Grace." (We were down in the bowels of the earth, and we decided to "make contact" with Someone who cared. That sort of saved that cave for me. I was moved, and when I'm in a cramped space, I like that.) After the singing, we all wriggled out into the daylight a little happier, I suppose.

***

But it seems to me that there is a tragedy in removing all doubt, in solving every mystery, in digging into corners, in running things to ground, in zooming in for the close-ups. You sacrifice anticipation, intrigue, suspense, and wonder—when you absolutely must know everything. The journey, it turns out, is often more wonderful than the destination; the imagined is often more exciting than the reality. The tug of curiosity can be interpreted as magnetism—or is it gravity? People cannot seem to accept a shadow as a place worth preserving: we have to shift the light and probe every dark corner, reveal all, remove the doubt, and the wonder. Very human, but tragic.

What if that room in the forest is just a place where trees decided not to grow?—or that big black spot on that distant cliff: what if it is not a cave but a shadow?—what if there is nothing but fog out there in the fog?—what if that old road leads to nothing but a rotted stump? what if that cry in the night was just the wind moving the clothesline, raking a zipper across the propane tank?—what if a cave is just a cave and, God forbid, a barn is just a barn? What about potential? What about The Possible? What about Hope?

***

I may be dragged off the road someday soon, across that little field, and into that old barn. That could happen. People around me are bored, and they have to reach into holes where there may be snakes, snorkel to the bottom of old swimming holes, break open rocks, climb all the peaks and burrow into the ground, and know everything for sure, beyond the shadow of a doubt. They are that way about Nature, themselves, God, study, their friends, their cars, their food, beauty, love, everything. They can't resist that old barn for long.

I like it MY way. I like to think that old barn is a mystic place, full of limitless potential and memory and wonder and stories. Each time I drive by, I feel the pull, and I know that someday I will go, on my own, into that sanctuary—in there where the outlaw hid, where the ruined farmer hanged himself, where the lovers were caught, where the little goat was born on Christmas Eve, where the sheriff was held hostage, where the Confederates hid the Spanish gold, and where the milkmaid fed the kittens on a dark and stormy night. Someday. Someday soon.

I am saving the old barn for that moment. If nothing is there, I'm going to lie about it.

Art by Scott Baldassari.

RIDE-ALONG

I discovered that Wifey and I were playing at something that to others was a life-and-death struggle. Here we were, off in the mountains after lives and careers in the thick of things—enjoying a degree of self-imposed isolation, marveling at the progression of the seasons, the aging of the hills themselves, the slow pace of people and traffic and time, dabbling at "work" and "survival" and "citizenship"just for the exercise—and others around us were very seriously engaged in the real thing. We knew that our truth was not everyone's truth.

I secretly thought it would be the same with aging. Somehow, I would have a choice in my degree of participation in this activity. >From the comfort of my forty-year-old self-image, I would dabble in senility, in graying, in "crippling up," in "doddering," then return to my sanctuary—and the others would just have to go through it for real. Youth would arrive and infuse my account, unnoticed, forever, and I would be sympathetic and kind, and secretly immune. (I told no one of this advantage, of course, because I am not a trouble-maker, and I can only account for myself. And I did not wish to disillusion the others.) Yeah, right.

***

I decided to attempt a "ride-along" on a "Meals-on-Wheels" type of foray with a man I knew down at the Senior Center. He (as well as others) logged hundreds of miles on some of the roughest roads in North America to deliver meals to shut-ins in the remote parts of the county—along with a smile, a little encouragement, some human contact. I considered the man a saint, and I wanted to witness his work. I made it clear up front that I was a visitor, and that I could not be a dependable substitute or replacement for such a man, ever. What I wanted was an education.

I went to the lady in charge, and she smiled and referred me to the other lady—the one who signed me up with the Center in the first place. These people are crafty, and they have a communication system we common folk do not comprehend.

"Hi," she said as I walked up to her desk. "Hear you want to become a driver for us!"

"Not me. I want to just ride along to see what the guys go through. Not entertainment—just curiosity."

"Spreading your wings, huh?"

"I don't want to spread anything, I just want to..."

"You'll have to fill out these papers," she said. And she produced a four inch thick pile of menacing-looking papers.

"My God," I said. "All I want is to..."

"Yeah. Okay. You got a pen? Is your insurance paid up? All your shots current?"

"Sure." I looked at the pile of papers, and I remembered being a drone of the huge school district in the city. Papers depressed me. This Senior Center was hooked up with the government. Bleak outlook!

"Be sure to take notes. It'll be an eye opener."

I gasped. I felt as if a huge wet mattress had been dropped on me. Papers! I knew that I didn't want the ride-along that bad. Now I needed a way to withdraw my request.

Then she grabbed up the papers and tossed the whole pile onto a desk top along the wall behind her. "Gotcha!" she said.

"What about the papers?"

"Just kidding. I hate papers. But, you shoulda seen your face." And she howled, and the other lady came in and howled, too—they laughed until they had to lean on each other to stand up. I heard other laughter down the hall. I may have released a faint smile. I don't remember. I doubt it, though. And they laughed at whatever I did! I suppose it was a good joke. And here I thought this was going to be serious.

***

Anyway, my wish was granted, and one morning in autumn I zoomed down to the Senior Center and hopped aboard the van that carried the vital cargo. The driver was a Viet Nam veteran, and he had my deep respect from the word go. He looked tough and capable. He had taken my place in that mess over there, personally, as far as I was concerned. Certainly some man went over there and put his life on the line in the war that could have been my war, while I taught English here at home. I hope I taught well, but I know I will never catch up.

The idea was that we would go out to the immobile people, the shut-ins, the isolated, the infirm, the needy, and deliver each of them a meal. It's done everywhere, rural and urban, and I wanted to know about it. I could visit old age, and return at the end of the day, like with a river float or a picnic or a hike, right? A simple plan.

A few feet off any paved surface in our area lay all the challenge a car would ever want to face, but the van we used was up to the job. Each jolt brought visions of brake jobs and suspension problems and tire shredding. I could imagine winter coming in with other problems. I thought about my pathetic little truck—and about commitment, then the long, crooked, rough road, cliffs left and right, no pull-out, no turn-around, one lane. One-way. The driver took it all in stride, and we went to places I had heard about but had never seen, or felt. The details were noisy, rough, bruising, brutal, and largely a blur, but a daily reality to those who lived there full time. We encountered many grateful older folks, and we delivered the meals, some smiles and waves and caring human voices: quick little visits, as planned.

We hit the widow Lydia Chesterton's place just before noon— out there somewhere I don't think I could ever find again. The sun was shining, the temperature was cool, the air was just drinkable! It was a golden Ozark Mountain day. The road past her outpost had a powdery dust on it about two inches thick, and when a car went through it fast, there was a formidable cloud. The foliage close on both sides of the road was powdered to a light gray.

We raised our own cloud, of course, as we approached and

pulled into the yard. It was a log cabin, rather old, and there was some weed whacking needed, hours and hours of repairs and painting, trimming, and hauling. An old rusty car was half hidden in a pile of brush, and there were a few cats running around. There were tires, and back in the brush, old appliances. I could imagine literally years of "projects" on this place. Lydia came out on the porch immediately.

"Look at that old fool," she scolded, waving toward the road. "Drivin' like a maniac! Look at that dust flyin'!" About eighty-five years old, I'd say—big smile, long floral dress, scarf wrapping her remaining white hair, weathered look generally, rugged shoes, over-sized knit sweater (over the dress, unbuttoned), rust-colored.

"Howdy, Mrs. Chesterton. How are you getting along?" said the driver.

"Nothin' wrong with me," Lydia Chesterton said, her eyes bright and merry. "But look at that old fool!"

I looked toward the road, about forty yards away, and I saw no one, no traffic. Our dust cloud had blown away, and there was nobody on the road. I insist.

The driver did not look. He just made sure that the meal was placed in Lydia's hands.

"Sure is a nice day, isn't it?" he said to her.

"Lovely day. We get some of the best days at this time of year. Gonna be a rough winter, though. Wooly worms is fat. Lots o' nuts a-fallin' down. Gonna be rough." I believed her.

"Well, we'll try to keep the meals comin'," assured the driver, "weather or not."

"Look at that! That old fool's gonna break his neck! Drivin' that old red car down these sorry roads so fast! Mark my words!"

I went for it again. I looked all up and down that road, searching for a red car, an old fool, a dust cloud, something. But I could see no one. Then I got it, and I felt sad and silly at the same time.

"Look out! He's gonna hit the tree! Oh, my God! He's just like a kid—a stupid kid!" And Lydia lived through some sort of crisis right there—totally involved in something only she was seeing on the road, something she really cared about.

"Well, if you just go inside and sit down at the kitchen table and get into this food, maybe everything will be all right," said the driver. "You'll just get all upset if you stay out here on the porch. It's gonna be all right."

"Yeah, it'll be all right. Jim, what the hell are you doin' over here? Ain't your mama got any control of you no more?" She was looking at me., and I felt her gaze, and her smile. She had been strong in her day. She had run things.

"Oh, I'm just tryin' to help out a little today," I said. I was willing to be Jim, but I was ready to leave, too.

"Well, look out! That old sucker in that red car might smack into yuh!" She waved her arms and actually cackled. Well, she laughed. Cackled is an unkind word.

"We'll just try to stay out of his way," I ventured.

"We'll be all right, Lydia," said the driver. "Enjoy your meal. We've gotta go. See you tomorrow. Got a long way to go."

"I keep tellin' him that the screen door is a-hangin' by a thread and he needs to shoot off a mess of them ground hogs, but he's got to be out there with that sorry car." But still, the smile.

"It'll all be okay, Mrs. Chesterton," said the driver, starting the motor of the van.

And we escaped. I said nothing as the driver turned us around and got us back out onto the dusty road. I guess I knew what was happening.

"Old Lydia there," said the driver about a quarter of a mile down the road, "She has a little problem. Near as I can tell, that's her dead husband out there drivin' up and down that road. She sees him, but nobody else does. Ghost, I guess, or memory."

"Hmmm. Did he die in a car crash out here somewhere?"

"Naw. He just got old, and they came for him with the helicopter one day, and he died in the hospital in Mountain Home. Few years back."

"But the car. All this driving up and down...?"

"No car. There's an old red one in the brush pile by the house, but nobody sees what she sees. Oh, and Jim? He was the neighbor boy, I think—back in the seventies."

"How can she survive out here? Will she really be all right?"

"It's a matter of time. Someday before too long she'll have to come to town. She has family. Right now she won't move—has her memories, doesn't want to give up yet. Raised her kids there. Her old family place—ancestors buried out back. Goin' on all over the hills. Matter of time."

***

That was what I wanted to know about, I guess. This was time travel, in a way. Someday, well down the line, I hoped, Wifey would be out there along the road, and a van would come, and maybe she would remember an "old fool" with a little flat hat—out there banging ice off the mail box, or lugging trash out to the burning barrel, or riding along on the lawn tractor (on two wheels), maybe getting mad and hurling a hammer into the woods, or some other mundane nonsense. Maybe she would mutter to strangers something about *my* little cloud of dust, my disturbance, my wrinkle in the fabric of time. Who knows?

I did not consider it madness—what Old Lydia Chesterton was going through—but a degree of awareness. Maybe some part of her husband was indeed hovering out there—orbiting—floating by in each cloud of dust—waiting for her. Where else would he be? Where else would I be?

At the end of the day, I was ready to admit that this old age journey was more than a mere prospect. It was up ahead there, in sight, right in the middle of the rough road, with cliffs on both sides, no pull-out or turn-around. It was time to learn to expect it and respect it and accept it, and smile.

INTIMATIONS OF CABIN FEVER

There is a tiny season: a lull, a pause in mid-September, when Nature seems to toss aside the Dog Days of August and very slowly experiment with Autumn. A few strokes of her brush here and there—a dab of brilliant red on the otherwise subtle-toned shrub or tree, the first tentative yellows on the black walnut leaves, an emergence of sumac fire!—and the late wild flowers that have spent the summer as weeds: all of it seems preliminary and undecided, separate from the deep bold green of wearying summer as well as the certain glory of the turning of the leaves, but loaded with excitement.

One year, I felt it especially strongly as I was enduring another birthday and the accompanying remorse/gratitude orgy. (I did not like being older, but the alternative, as my students used to say, "sucked out loud.") Suddenly it was all around us, everywhere—a whole little season of subtle, daily changes everywhere—high up on the ridges, but in the deepest valleys too, down along the Buffalo, Big Creek, Spider Creek, Hurricane Creek, and on the cliff walls, and along the old logging roads and the animal trails. Although we could see it from our window, Wifey insisted on deeper involvement.

I always liked Emily Dickinson's way. "A clover and a bee, and reverie" would get it for me. I did not have to examine every blade of grass to comprehend a prairie, and I did not have to walk twenty miles and turn over every rock to appreciate the Ozarks. Lazy, I guess. But this tiny season—before the almost painful dazzle of Fall—before the first frost, when it's already too cold for the old swimming hole, and the kids are cooped up in school, and the wild places are devoid of tourists because the rivers are slow and shallow and therefore empty of canoes—this hesitation in the affairs of Nature had to be acknowledged: witnessed. I knew that in my poet's heart. I am sensitive, damn it. Everybody in my family was sensitive, always.

Truth be told, Wifey and one of her friends (Lacy) dragged me out to a bluff in a nearby swatch of wilderness for a hefty hike and some cave exploration. It was habitual with The Maker, while working on our part of His project, to erect strings of cliffs perforated with cave entrances leading to warrens—honeycombs—networks of caverns, extending for miles. The openings at the bases of the cliffs fire the imagination of some of us, and invite many others to enter and get lost and learn to appreciate bears and snakes and blind, slippery, colorless, crawly critters. I went *there* with *them* and saw *that.*

It is impossible to look at all those caves without thinking about ancient man. He must have taken shelter there—lived there—spent the winter—created a plethora of artifacts to be dug up later, etc.

At some time, I slipped my leash, and temporarily escaped my abductors. While I was sprawled on a giant slab of rock in front of an impressive alcove, taking a few rays of September sun and imagining how it might have been for the unsuspecting passer-by eons ago when that slab of rock fell out of the face of the cliff (and what he must be doing now, flattened there under the rock, starving and thirsty, no doubt), I got to looking at the immediate cave area along the base of the bluff. Wifey and Lacy had disappeared inside a cave, of course, and were probably turning over rocks in there, searching, or measuring for curtains or carpet or something. (I never understood women.) I was meditating, if you will, and dozing, perhaps, and definitely taking the crisp outdoor air—outside the cave there. Too soon they would discover my escape.

Anyway, the place started looking more and more like a system of dwellings—homes—apartments. Years before, we had scrambled through cave dwellings out west, in cliffs like these, and I began feeling Them now: the Ancient Ones, like those folks out there in Colorado, Utah, New Mexico, Arizona, Nevada...

Before long I rolled the whole fantasy back into pre-history but also ahead into winter—or I fell asleep there on that rock—or another rock fell on my head—I don't know for sure. But soon I had a pair of them, husband and wife, right there in the cave near me, and it was winter, and there was a three-inch coat of ice everywhere outside (an Ozark phenomenon), and just enough snow on top of that to shut the whole place down and confine everyone to quarters: a complete, modern Ozark winter, but with the original residents of the county.

***

"Do you think I look fat in this buckskin dress?" asked Moon Dove, the wife image of the cave. (Long, smoked, braided gray hair, leather outfit and skin, etc.)

"Huh?" said the old warrior, Spotted Liver. He was busily scratching a pictograph in the black soot of the cave wall, preoccupied.

"You heard me: Does this buckskin make me look fat? You never listen."

"You look slim enough for all practical purposes," grunted Hubby. (Retired, plump, very faded war paint, blanket, etc.)

"What is that supposed to mean?"

"You look fine, Moon Dove. All the braves say so, even the young ones. Hand me a slice of that jerky, will yuh?" (There would be meat hanging around—getting smoked, probably.)

"The dress feels tight. I want your opinion. I want a real answer, not just 'You look fine.'"

"If you're fat, don't blame the buckskin. And don't blame me." (Oh, I would never have said that! But this guy was a "brave.")

"I think it shrunk during that last dry spell," she said, tugging at the hips of the dress.

"I'll shoot you a bigger deer when the weather clears and we can get outside. Meanwhile, please pass the jerky."

I was impressed by the language. These two used prepositions, articles, and auxiliary verbs—none of this Tonto Talk they use in movies. This was a sophisticated fantasy.

"All you ever do, Spotted Liver, is sit around and snack! And someday you'll pay for it." Moon Dove threw some jerky at him.

"I sit around and *your* clothes get tight?" said Spotted Liver. "Seems unlikely to me."

"And I wish you would leave that wall alone. You can't draw a turkey anyway, and your elk look like beavers. And your humans! Forget it!"

"Hey, what do you want from me, photo realism? I'm going for something a little abstract here."

"Oh, it's abstract, all right. Do landscapes, though: your anatomy just bites."

"I am making a statement, a declaration. I'm baring my soul."

"Well, it doesn't flow. Are you trying for pictures, or are you writing? I can't tell."

"A little of both. Maybe someday they'll move some people in here who have an alphabet. Meanwhile, I scratch the wall. Nothing is chiseled in stone here. Hey! Chiseled in stone. I like that."

"I can hardly wait. You can't even make a decent tomahawk, and you want to chisel something in stone." Nasty and scornful like that. Women. Go figure.

"A man gets no respect in his own cave! I'll have you know that some in the tribe like my cave drawings just fine. Pictographs, they call 'em."

"A thousand years from now, people will find these walls and wonder how we lived if we were that ugly." Indeed, Moon Dove's dress had identifiable beaded depictions, and the wall etchings of Spotted Liver "sucked out loud"—to quote the classics.

"Women! You are so ungrateful! All those years of hunting and fishing and fighting, and what does it get me now that I'm old?"

"Huh! I should be grateful, I suppose, for being holed up in a cave getting my brains smoked all winter! I warned you. I saw the wooly worm! I saw all the acorns and walnuts! I told you it would be a hard winter and that we should go to the Gulf for the winter months. But No! You never listen."

"The fur on the beavers and coons was thin! How was I to know?"

"I told you. There were signs. You're just like your mother—can't tell you anything!"

"You leave my mother out of this! That woman was a saint! And *she* could cook."

Moon Dove leaped to her feet and walked right through the fire toward her husband. I could have warned him. You don't mess around with a wife's cooking.

"What is wrong with my cooking?" she bellowed.

"You don't know either?" he retorted.

"Don't go there, Spotted Liver," I yelled; but of course, I was too late, and they couldn't hear me anyway. (Time-Warp Rules.) They squared off in the middle of the cave.

"You are disorganized and messy," Moon Dove fired.

"You are obsessive compulsive," Spotted Liver pulled up from somewhere.

"You can't find anything!" she shouted, tossing a piece of firewood at him.

"You can get lost in a tepee!" he countered, tossing the wood on the fire.

"You are too proud to ask for directions when lost!" Moon Dove did not care that this tidbit did not fit in. She stood there, arms akimbo, glaring.

"I'm not the one running around lost all the time!" Spotted Liver wagged his finger in a circle at his temple—an ancient sign for "You're addled and crazy."

"Your mama was a Kickapoo," Moon Dove charged.

"Yours was an Ojibwa!"

"You drove the children away from our home!"

"They ran away from your nagging and your cooking!"

Moon Dove grabbed up a basket of arrowheads the two of them had been making all winter and dumped them over Spotted Liver's head. (That's probably why the landscape is littered with arrowheads today. I always wondered how they lost so many of them. The shops are full of them.) Then she threw axes and spear heads at him. Quite a spat, really.

"Now calm down," said Spotted Liver, ducking and dodging. "We have a contract: you belong to me as long as the grasses grow and the rivers flow."

"But in this tribe the women own everything and treaties mean nothing," Moon Dove shot back, whacking him with a big stick. "And if you continue speaking with a forked tongue, you'll end up with a wounded knee, and I'll do a stomp dance right on your tom-tom, and you'll have your own personal Trail of Tears—and I'll *STILL* get all the wampum *and* our interest in the casino..."

***

Well, it got just dumb then, and I screamed and woke myself up. I found myself right there on the big slab of rock along the cliffs, cold, and quite alone, but sweating. I was dazed and a little embarrassed, and I looked around to see if anyone had witnessed my outburst. Wifey and Lacy were just emerging from the cave, giggling and gossiping, probably about their inept, doddering husbands.

"Look," chirped Wifey. "I found three arrowheads, inside the cave, and there are some drawings on the wall—of chickens and rats, I think."

"Naw, they're turkeys and elk."

"How would you know? You wouldn't even go into the cave."

"Well, that's a long story," I said.

I explained most of it to them as Wifey drove the three of us home. Wifey's friend chuckled once, Wifey yawned, and they both lost interest completely at about McElroy Gap, and started exchanging recipes. Then I fell into the view and lost my train of thought.

I don't intend to tell anybody else about that incident. It's probably about something deeply psychological that could get me into a lot of trouble. These things are never simple.

JURY DUTY

On April 15, earlier that year, a Ford pick-up truck had crossed Jasper bridge heading south and had hit a PT Cruiser a glancing blow, right there in front of The Junction—a gas station/mini-mart, if not the heart of town, certainly a vital organ. The scene was cleared in a few minutes, really, and the disruption was minimal.

A few months later, there I was at the trial. When you are tapped for jury duty in our neck of the woods, you might get in on two or three trials, depending on how busy things are at the county courthouse, the size of the jury pool, and luck. I did not consider myself unlucky to be on jury duty. I have a very deep sense of civic responsibility. Really. Besides, I needed the four dollars.

In the city, the jury pool was huge, and if I was actually impaneled, I felt special. There was a joke about jury duty: that a person really ought to be smart enough to avoid it altogether. But, for some reason, I liked it. It was time away from the humdrum of work; it was life in the big city—downtown, in the middle of things; it was involvement in The Process; it was variety—potential adventure; and it was my civic duty. But, most of all, it was potential debate.

Trouble was, I was invariably Foreman of the Jury—a moderator, not a debater. We would go from the courtroom into the jury room, and the others would take one look at my glasses and elect me foreman immediately—over and over, every time—even when, on one occasion, I foxed them and went directly to the restroom. I took my time, flushed, came out, and found out I was foreman. Again. Elected in absentia. I griped about that a lot, but secretly I felt important. (There's a lot of that going around.)

But this time, in the small town environment, I sat on the jury, and nobody gave me a second look when it came to picking a foreman. We were not dressed for church, but we were not outfitted for work or hunting either. It was court. There was a muscular girl with great personal authority (jeans, good tough arms, tan, healthy glow, about 35), and we foisted it off on her immediately. It was beautiful. I was off the hook. I relaxed, quite happy, really. I could debate this time. I was satisfied. Really.

Well, I was, too, satisfied! No bitterness in me at all. I did not feel slighted. Shut up.

In the courtroom we had heard the legal evidence, and most of us had a pretty good idea of what had happened. The PT Cruiser, driven by Meg Clausen, had pulled out onto Highway Seven, right in front of the Ford pick-up, driven by Freddy Wainwright. Meg had Billy Clausen, her pierced, tattoed, anti-social, Gothed-out son with her, and Freddy had picked up Old Zeke out by Bob's Market and was giving him a ride through town. Meg was uninjured, Freddy and Zeke were just shaken up a little, but Billy had been shooting the finger at someone at the gas pump at The Junction, and his hand and forearm were smashed up just enough to evoke screams and terrible rhetoric, and impressive scars. No two ways about it, though: Meg had goofed up. I insist.

Oh, there was a "story" in the paper—well, an item in the Sheriff's Log: "Deputies responded to accident scene in Jasper. Cleared." The judge denied a motion for a Change of Venue. Perspective is important.

And you can't blame the lawyers: it's their job to muddy the waters and be repetitious and obtuse. And it's the judge's job to try to keep things as technically honest and aboveboard as feasible—given the political climate, the time frame, the money, yada yada yada. We went through all of that. The trial was over, and it was time to decide. Meg and her boy wanted money for pain and suffering, psychological damage, loss of mobility, diminished capacity, medical expenses, car damage, negligence, and all that. We would decide.

The judge always admonishes the jury that it must consider only the evidence brought forth in the trial. Even a printed note to us scolded us in advance: only what we've talked about in court can be considered. The foreman was required to read that to the rest of us. (She didn't read it as well as I would have, but she got it out there.) Naturally, we immediately tossed that aside and proceeded.

"I think there should be a flashing yellow light at The Junction," said Marvin Something-Or-Other—I never did know his last name (new guy like me, only about a dozen years in the hills, denim and flannel). "A caution light."

"You put one up," said The Smoker, "and I'll shoot it down. We don't need no traffic lights in this county. Never have, never will."

"But there isn't one traffic light in the whole county. I'm just talkin' about a flashing amber caution light..."

"Yeah," said The Smoker, "something to show the grandchildren..." He was sucking on a pencil. (Tall man, lots of denim, gray pony tail, bandana.)

"That was not an option mentioned in court," I said. "We have to stick to what was said in court."

The Foreperson gave me a look, and I slid back in my chair and folded my hands in my lap. Everyone present stared at me. I had overstepped. I had only been in the hills for five years at the time.

"We have to decide whose fault the accident was," the Foreperson said firmly. "That is all we have to decide."

"I say we vote right now," said The Smoker, "and get out of here." He was in need.

The Reader (loose-fitting, feminine clothes—casual comfort all the way—Penney's, I think) sat at one corner of the large table in the jury room, reading a book, chewing gum, and seemingly ignoring the rest of us. (She was like that even at pie suppers.) Next to her was a Hispanic guy (shirt & tie, Dockers) who turned out to be a machine shop owner/manufacturer with a little shop out in the hills. He was unusual because there were few Hispanic guys around in the county at that time. Bouncing off the wall and around the room was a friend of mine—and everyone, I guess, everyone in town—who was simply not small room material. She was already bored and restless, leaping about (denim, tennis shoes, white socks, short hair). The Statue was next to me—a stiff, immobile lady who later turned out to be distantly related to both drivers (dark clothes, I think—but some red). There was another older lady, also, who wisely said nothing at first—as I should have.

But it was The Gadfly (all urban cowboy) who spoke. "It won't look good if we vote right now. We need to tread water for a while, then I say we just convict this maniac with the pick-up and throw his butt in jail."

I started to speak, but I held my tongue. The Foreperson said, "Nobody goes to jail. We just say whose fault the accident was, say who pays, and we're outa here."

"How do we know it wasn't attempted murder," said The Gadfly, "or gross negligence or malfeasance without habeas corpus—or worse!"

"Yeah—that obnoxious kid *was* hurt," someone blurted.

"I hate that kid. He tried to sell me a bunch of blackberries one time. I hate blackberries. Did us all a favor mangling that kid's 'finger' hand," the gruff-sounding old lady said (sorta tough lace). I could tell she had seen enough of that particular finger. I imagined her knitting, cackling, "Guillotine, guillotine!"

"Remember the cell phone," said The Artist quietly. (The Artist was always quiet. Landscape painter.)

"What cell phone?" said The Gadfly.

"Meg was talking on a cell phone when the crash happened. She is right handed. She was hit from the right side. Maybe she couldn't see."

"Huh! We got us a detective here," sneered The Gadfly.

"I just think her visibility might have been blocked," concluded The Artist. Having made his point, he leaned back. He was concerned with point-of-view, I noticed.

I was privately working on three little references: rotten kid, blackberries, and cell phone. I was wondering if this kid was the rat in Limestone Valley who had ripped off some of my berries! But that was another story from a long time ago. I tossed it aside.

"Wainwright should have known that Meg was gonna make that turn and head for the Post Office. She always goes there before she goes to Bob's Market, and everybody knows it! It was April 15, too. Income Tax had to be mailed. Mail? Post Office? Hello!" The Gadfly was tough in there—and probably right.

"And that would make it Freddy Wainwright's fault," said The Smoker. "Let's go home."

"Wait a minute," said the Foreperson. "Let's talk some more. Does anybody disagree with that thinking?"

"Seems like that would make it Meg's fault, I mean if she had a stop sign, like they said, and she didn't signal..." said Marvin. "Still, if we had a yellow light..."

"Not gonna be any light," screeched my bounding friend, from a window sill, I believe. "We're not gonna talk any more about the light. I'd shoot it out myself if you put one up. We have a tradition: no traffic lights. It was human error, that's all. The only good thing that happened was that sorry kid got his hand squashed like a bug—which served him right for shooting the rod..." Her voice trailed off, and everybody stared at her, and she settled into a chair, temporarily.

"Anybody else have feelings about this?"

A quiet old lady, whom I swear I had never seen before this gathering, raised her hand. The Foreperson nodded to her. "I object," she said simply.

"To what?" asked the Foreperson.

"Iraq," she said.

"Iraq?" asked the Foreperson.

"Yes. Stupid, stupid, stupid." She was wearing her good dress and her church hat with a little screen hanging down the front—and what looked like flies all over it.

"Well, thank you, but we can't handle that here. But thank you," said the Foreperson. I liked her for that. Compassionate.

The Statue then spoke. "I never liked the Wainwrights. Uppity, rich folks. Always git their way."

"That's not evidence," I said. I got kicked under the table, and for a while I thought Wifey had gotten into the room. Whoever kicked me was right, though. I was not Foreman. "Never mind," I said, "I withdraw my...uh...never mind."

The Foreperson then asked for further input in general. One person recalled that Meg had been in an accident back in '87, so this one must have been her fault, too. A pattern had developed. The shop owner from The Square said she had experienced trouble getting money out of Meg, but that Freddy was also an ass—and she didn't have much use for Wainwrights, and Old Zeke scared her to death. (Old Zeke did that to some folks.)

One guy, I forget which one, hated Fords, and, despite my humble status in the room, I myself mentioned something about PT Cruisers being the ugliest vehicles in the history of technology. (The Foreperson informed me that that was not evidence, and I agreed, cowering.) The Reader, without looking up out of her book, said that she hated red cars: that they reminded her of her divorce, and that she hated vehicles in general because she had been run down by an occupied baby stroller at Silver Dollar City.

The Gadfly suggested that we flip a coin for the verdict, but pointed out that we did have a woman driver to consider, and that should be enough right there. All women on the jury bristled. The Hispanic fellow spoke up in perfect English and said that the Ford driver reminded him of a liar that he used to know (now dead), and that anybody who would pick up a hitchhiker who looked like Old Zeke (a costumed character, self-invented, who had worked at Dogpatch USA in former times) was not to be trusted. Someone else countered that Wainwright had helped him change a tire once, long ago, on Mt. Sherman, and he couldn't be all bad. It surfaced also that the person at the gas pump wasn't "right in the head," and probably deserved the finger gesture, as did most members of his family!

I was relieved that actual legal evidence had been taken off the table. It was tedious, in the city, when we would get bogged down in facts and truth and such nonsense. Here, everybody knew everybody else (or was related), and we just logically knew who was the type of person who would be at fault. Even I, a "come here," knew what the important stuff was.

Meg's ignored stop sign on Highway 74 stayed ignored, but in the end, we cut straight to the core of the matter: Meg's lawyer was a petulant red-headed S.O.B. from Russellville, and we all hated him. He was from "Off," and he was sarcastic. And we hated Meg's damned kid, too, more than we hated the Wainwrights for being successful. 'Nuff said.

It amused me that we got the verdict right, even without my expert leadership as foreman. Meg's insurance company paid, the kid's arm healed (but he has one frozen finger now, forever in "salute" mode), and Old Zeke is thinking about a whiplash claim, retroactively. (He liked court, he told me: said he wouldn't mind spending a few days there.)

***

I believe in the jury system, I really do. We would have ferreted out the right murderer, if necessary, or the culpable pedophile priest, or the crooked CEO, or the guilty widow or heiress. You put twelve diverse people into a room and present them with the prospect of staying there with each other, and you get some justice in a real hurry. I believe that. I really, really do. (As an afterthought, we agreed to something else: we could have hooked the county for a meal if we had delayed a little. But The Smoker would never have made it.)

I get along well with the muscular girl now. I respect her. I would give her a hug. Still, I believe the Foreman of the Jury should be a distinguished person—with experience, dignity, and poise—and big glasses.

CANOE TRACKS

Rick Roller, as far as I was concerned, was the Ozark Distributor, the District Manager, the Ayatolla, Sultan, and Royal Omnipotent High Potentate Supreme of Adult Onset Attention Deficit Hyperactivity Disorder. He roved the back roads of the county all summer on an All-Terrain Vehicle (ATV): day after day, good weather and bad, alone and accompanied. He was a wild man, a phenomenon, and a hoot.

His own wife rode with him until they had seen every waterfall and boulder in the county; *my* wife rode with him until they had seen every puddle and pebble; two other free-spirited women rode with him and visited every tree, cliff, and cave. He wore out two or three guys, too. Then they shuffled the passenger list, and Rick toured all of it again, until all of them had experienced every remote alcove, every hollow stump, every rivulet and spring and mossy rock, forever and ever, world without end, amen.

Naturally, I was exhausted—just knowing about it. I am a quick study (mind like a steel trap, etc.), and to me a rock is a rock and a tree is a tree and a trickle makes me want to tinkle, and I "get it" fast. I do not need to examine every grain of sand in a desert to get the concept. Nevertheless, one day I went along—out there with them—on a junket into the wilderness. And that is when I learned about canoe tracks.

***

Down along the Buffalo National River (National by act of Congress), in deep, late summer especially, things dry up, and the riverbed becomes a rocky field with a small creek beside it. Rick was attracted to that—perhaps because he was compelled to go on foot where others had been in canoes (just as he would need to dive or climb to places without air, or drive cars over ground too rough for bulldozers, or fly without wings to sea caves in outer space). But also, he was attracted to it because every rock—thousands at any glance—could be turned over and examined, perhaps diagramed or photographed, or merely fondled, then stacked—or treated and released! Go figure. Rick had all day, so he would use up one site and then head upstream a mile to another. It was that sort of safari that I signed on for that day—with Wifey, Rick, Rick's wife Rita, and the free-spirited ladies.

We were all on foot and hopping along the dry riverbed when Rick suddenly stopped and called our attention to some green paint on a rock underfoot, then on another rock, and then on a row of rocks, ranging over a hundred feet. A dotted green line. And beside that trail, there was a red one, and a yellow one, and a brown.

"Huh," I thought, "paint smudges on rocks. My heart leaps up." (I have a flare for sarcasm.) But out loud, I said, "Gee, Gang—rocks!"

"Canoe tracks," said Rick Roller.

And I was finished with the sarcasm. I could see that when the river was up, canoes had zoomed through where we were standing, and in these shallows, they had scraped their bottoms on these rocks, losing a little paint. I could imagine all the colorful canoes, the squeals and the laughter, the splashing, the waving of paddles, the sun, the joy—of someone else's unforgettable moment: clear water, fresh air, no real worries, wonderful people from everywhere, a crazy quilt of life preservers and ice chests and bathing suits and towels of every brilliant color, lucky, healthy "floaters," gazing in wonder at these very cliffs. I could smell wet hair and suntan lotion, and I could see that goofy zinc oxide on pretty noses, and little kids with iridescent hats and float toys. Full-blown summer flooded in. The red canoe zoomed by to my right; the yellow went right between my legs (yeah, I flinched); the green one came close behind, but probably later. The place was haunted by the giggling ghosts of tourists, out-of-control and winging it, and happy.

And they were as unaware of me as I had been of them. They probably never considered that they could be tracked—trailed—followed by people like us on foot—someday. They probably thought they had blown through there without leaving a mark. It was not mere paint-streaked rocks I was examining with Rick, it was the remains of someone's indelible day on the river.

Rick grinned as the message struck home; then he bounded off downstream.

I sat down, and listened, and remembered a day of my own, and, in re-living that, I made a better day of the one I was living presently. The others wandered off, getting whatever they get out of such revelations. And I wondered if anyone screaming through there in a canoe some incredible day in the future would feel traces of me.

***

So, now I know about canoe tracks. I don't know if the knowledge will ever be useful. Maybe it's like Algebra. (Look for it on your IRS forms.) Maybe it's like nominative absolutes and retained objects. (Nobody cares.) Maybe it's too obscure to be of value. Or maybe it's like whatever it is that makes little boys climb trees, snoop in cupboards and closets, poke sticks into holes. Maybe it's a reminder that there are levels of awareness—parallel scenarios—that we must try to notice. But I am glad that I have become aware of canoe tracks.

Rick Roller might be a bit much, but I think he's onto something. He is not dragging people "out there," he is leading them. I keep thinking of what a great teacher he would have been. He is capable of making a visit to a dry, post-season canoe river into an episode, an intrigue, an adventure.

That may have been him just now. Something just shrieked by on Scenic Byway Seven, and the tourist season is over. And Rick's out there somewhere. He just needs to be understood. Perhaps restrained.

LOTTERY DREAMS

The citizens had voted many times, and it was official: no gambling would be allowed in our state. And the county had made it clear that alcohol was not going to be sold or manufactured within its borders (legally, in the light of day). Marijuana and meth were against the law everywhere. Naturally, the border region to our north was a busy strategic area.

Emissaries from our community ran regular routes up across the border into Missouri to purchase lottery tickets for organized pools of locals (an ecological consideration, of course: no use sending all those vehicles when one car stuffed with buyers could take care of the buy). These emissaries insulated the actual buyers from the "sin."

But the lottery was, after all, not *really* gambling. Sometimes, when there was a hundred million dollars on the line, it would be mentioned on TV that the odds were something like 2 billion-to-one against you, and that's not really gambling. In gambling, you have a chance. Nevertheless, there were takers—legions of them. Also, the little scratch cards were popular stocking-stuffers at Christmas. We knew all about the lottery, but it was an "Order-In" sort of thing. Harmless, like Bingo.

Naturally, a few bottles of spiritus fermenti could be purchased over the same counter there on the Missouri border It was legal to bring some alcohol across the line—not enough to sell, mind you, but enough for personal use: medicinal, ceremonial, etc. Delicate situation. The emissaries would take care of some of that, too. We had "wet" counties in the state, but in our county, we had to "Order In." We had voted.

Since the marijuana and meth-amphetamines were illegal

everywhere, the border was not a factor with that. Our rich national forest and wilderness areas—a great percentage of our county—provided cover for all of that. The sheriff and his men had employment (bad guys to chase), the little helicopter the authorities unloaded from a truck down at the fair grounds patrolled the wooded hills with a purpose (crop control), and that made the newspaper and the courthouse viable, too (something to write about, and something to have trials about). One has to assume, however, that those with un-prescribed "needs" did not have to "Order In."

All of it made the churches all the more necessary. Symbiosis, Gang! The churches were officially against all of it, and said so every Sunday, and everybody knew the rules. Most people, however, had an understanding of Bingo, and especially the lottery.

***

"If'n I win the hundred million tonight," said Old Zeke, "that li'l waitress is gonna be able to quit her job—'cuz I'm gonna give her the tip of her life."

"Shame, too," said Cowboy Jess, "because *I'm* a-gonna win it. And I'm a-gonna put good teeth in every head in the county. Then I'm a-gonna run *off* with that waitress!"

"Huh. You wouldn't know what to do with her," said Zeke.

"I could read books and find out. Lord knows I don't remember anything."

Well, there was a little laughter at the table at the Ozark Café. The lottery—the Power Ball option—was "up there," and there were lots of takers and lots of talkers. It was a time for speculation. It was coffee for all of them, and Diet Coke for me. (We liked the refills.) (This was a meeting that had its roots in the old Mockingbird Hill Café a few years back: sort of a gathering of self-apotheosized philosophers. It was an echo of a one-time institution.)

"I never personally participate in the lottery," rasped Old Clem, "until it reaches seventy-five millions. Then, and only then, will I give up my dollar. Gambling offends my delicate sensibilities, but a man has to be social." His voice rattled dishes on the table.

Double-Dog Darrell was on the scene, of course, and he was in a petulant mood. "You fools ought to be ashamed of yourselves. You put perfectly good money into a thing like that? Like pourin' money down a rat hole. I am above all of it!"

"What *are* your numbers this week?" asked Clem, because everybody was onto Double-Dog's game. He was a faithful lottery parishioner, whenever he could afford it.

"I run the same numbers every week. You know that," said Double-Dog, without blinking, "And the waitress? She's mine." Delusions of grandeur. Appropriate jeering all around.

I was not about to comment on the waitress, because, unlike the others, I was married. Any comment about the waitress from me would have started terrible rumors or caused hysterical laughter— both hard to handle—and Wifey would have killed me. Slowly, very slowly. If not out of hatred, certainly out of chagrin. Besides, I hardly noticed that waitress. I insist.

Justin Kase, resident poet, sat among us, wielding his mighty pen, as usual, occasionally lifting his gaze from his immortal notebook and striking his patented reading pose. We waited for our cue.

"How do you guys get those lottery tickets every week? I don't get up to the border that much," I told the gang.

"The Syndicate," Old Clem rattled. (He had been unable to find out what had happened to his voice, but a year ago he had suddenly started sounding like "jake" brakes.)

"Well, how do I get in touch with this syndicate? I guess I could afford one ticket, and I could use the hundred million myself."

"It's a secret society," said Old Zeke. "Very mysterious. If we told you, we'd have to kill you." Zeke had a flare for melodrama, and cliché.

"Yeah, right."

"Honest to God," said Double-Dog Darrell, looking at me in disgust, "you have got to be the last fool in the county to figure this out. But don't you worry about a thing—your wife has had you in this Power Ball thing for three weeks. Ticket for you and ticket for her, like clockwork."

"Aha!" I said, "*You* are in The Syndicate."

"She said that if she won she was gonna have your place bulldozed into the canyon and replaced by a big log cabin," said Cowboy Jess.

"Works for me," I muttered. "Six solid years of work, shoved into the canyon. Why not?" I had no doubt that Wifey could *run* such a syndicate if she wanted to. She had been doing a few little secret transactions lately—since receiving her legacy (S.S.S. Direct Deposits). Another milestone.

At that moment, Justin Kase raised up and gave the significant look. Our cue. We turned to him and listened. He rose, tossed his scarf over his shoulder. The wind absolutely howled, I insist.

'Twas Power Ball,
And that was all!
We gathered up our order
(Our money Pool)
And paid our "mule,"
And sent him to the border!

We applauded and heaped praise upon the poet. Privately, I thought, "That man is a genius."

"What happens if *you* win?" Zeke asked me as The Poet sat down.

"A hundred million? First, I would go up to Springfield and find that TV used car salesman with the high, tinny voice, and pay him to get off the air forever. Or I'd have him hit, or his voice trained, or his throat cut. Then I'd replace the house all the way, go solar, hire ten fine Mexican gardeners to landscape the place for me, and employ a staff of about eight maids and butlers to cater to our whims. And I'd have a nice little cabin out back."

"What's the cabin for?" asked Jess.

"That waitress."

***

Turned out Rick Roller was the courier for The Syndicate. Why not? He was in and out of four states twice a week anyway on his ATV or dirt bike or "hawg." The Syndicate capitalized on his hyperactivity, and it was good for everyone. I found that out later from Wifey as I quizzed her about the lottery tickets. Bingo, and the lottery, too? A bit rich for our blood.

And when we got serious, all of us at the cafe came up with wonderfully constructive things we would do with the hundred million: scholarships for polite, un-tattooed, respectful, un-pierced, straight, non-promiscuous, clean kids; facilities for the county's orphan pets; grants for the women's shelter, the nursing home, the Senior Center, and Meals-On-Wheels; a new set of tires for everyone in the county (it was too late for the roads, most felt). Oh, and a county helicopter for free emergency taxi service, and pizza delivery. Wonderful ideas. A passer-by, whom I knew from somewhere (I couldn't remember at first), said that we ought to put some thought into a traffic light at The Junction: a flashing yellow caution light. He was laughed out of the café, and Cowboy Jess offered to follow him out and beat him senseless. Then I remembered him from jury duty. Marvin Something-Or-Other. Pathetic, deluded individual.

The Poet rose again, and we focused intently. Justin threw his long scarf over his shoulder and stared at things far away. I thought I heard the wind, moaning, sighing, again.

"I sing of bird and bush and hill
And vale and peak and butte,
But when I win that hundred mill,
My pen will then fall mute!"

And we applauded, thinking the poem was certainly complete. But there was more. Justin Kase was inspired.

"I'm just a humble man of words:
I celebrate the dawn.
I write of sunrise, flowers and birds,
But if I win, I'm gone!"

Then he sat down. Certainly, it must have been poetry. I was ready for it to be poetry. Only deep inside me was there any doubt at all—a doubt I would never reveal. We applauded quietly and thought deep thoughts.

"I would open a liquor store," said Double-Dog Darrell suddenly, "right here on the square."

"But that's illegal," I warned. "You could end up in jail, and they'd shut it down and confiscate the stock. Real waste of money."

"But it would be an event!" said DDD. And he got that manic look he had mastered to terrify tourists (when he chose). "It would be Spectacle, High Drama, History—and very short! And I'd get to spend some time in the Historic Jasper Jail: legendary, unforgettable stuff. My Dungeon Diary would be a classic."

"The Dungeon Diary of Double-Dog Darrell," I muttered. "I can't stand it." And Justin Kase scribbled furiously.

"And the confiscated stock could be the basis for another little trustee/dispatcher picnic," said Old Zeke, calling back memories of a sheriff department mishap/scandal.

The waitress came to the table at that point, and there was reverent silence. Refills all around. It was re-fueling, pure and simple, and she murmured, "You boys need to keep up your strength." My Diet Coke got a refill, too, and I felt better. Murmured. The girl murmured. Quietly. Moist little red mouth. Slow eyes. There was a collective sigh, then silence. Quite a bit of silence.

"I would spend my hundred million on travel," said Cowboy Jess, after the respectful pause.

"I thought you told me you had been everywhere you wanted to go," said DDD. "You told me so—said you had done everything and been everywhere."

"Well, I have," said Cowboy Jess. "But I didn't say who would do the travelin'. I like it here, and I'm a-stayin' here. But there are people I would like to see travel. If I had serious bucks, I'd make sure some of these dipsticks woke up in foreign lands!"

"You'd have them kidnapped and sent away?" (I thought I should get the story straight.)

"I believe the word is Shanghaied. I'd have certain citizens Shanghaied—regularly. I would simply send them away. Annoying people. Stupid people. Lazy, cowardly, worthless people. Make a better place out of it around here."

"Well, I guess that would work," I said. "Sometimes you add, sometimes you subtract."

"You're gonna love Tibet," he said.

There was some laughter, but I didn't let it bother me. Much. I've always wanted to see Tibet anyway.

"I'll bring you some yak butter," I said after things died down.

"I'd buy up Dogpatch [defunct area theme park] and bring it back to life," said Old Zeke. "With a hundred million, I could bring the whole county back to life, and preserve the noble hillbilly traditions and skills—re-open the speak-easy in Mystic Cave—set 'em up to make baseball bats and hammer handles again in Lurton. I'd do some good, I tell yuh. There'd be jobs. Industry."

Old Zeke just wanted to fit in somewhere, and everything he had been a part of had disappeared. That's why he was pretty much a hermit—lived in the deepest boonies, way out there. He had been, and he remained, a costumed Dogpatch character—worthy of Al Capp himself. He had never forgiven the culprits who let Dogpatch USA fall to ruin. There were plenty of others like him in the county. Dogpatch was a sad story, and getting to be an old one.

The waitress finally floated over to us on a cloud of pink mist and let us know she had been listening. "When I win that hundred million," she said, sorta pouting, "I'm gonna just run away, and take all you boys with me."

You could hear every drop of coffee being poured. Nobody moved but the waitress. The Poet stilled his pen. Nobody breathed. Everybody waited. All of us got that faraway look in his eye—like the poet's dramatic gaze. When she replenished my Diet Coke, my ears turned red. (I always hated that.) I instinctively drew my legs back under my chair where they couldn't be kicked. But Wifey was nowhere around. I was on my own, and nobody was reading my mind.

***

Then I had a big epiphany: the lottery was all about dreams and fantasy and wild, desperate hope. And our mob? We were just a bunch of harmless old coots, spinning daydreams in a café, and ogling the waitress. (Well, those other guys were ogling her.) Just old men, dreaming. And it doesn't get any better than that. Everybody left that little gal a goodly tip later—probably thirty-five or forty cents. Apiece. She had earned every penny of it.

Life is good.

UP THERE

The gleaming house clinging to the very edge of one of the highest cliffs in the county was hardly a secret. In the Parthenon Valley you could see it clearly enough: a white rectangle way up top—hundreds of feet up, in fact, and almost leaning out there, like a suicide hoping to be talked down. It was so very public, really, for something that had obviously been built for privacy and exclusivity.

"Boy, I'll bet they have safety belts on the beds up there! Roll out of bed and drop for five minutes..." I ventured when I first saw it.

And I was not alone. Everyone seemed to have a dark, lame joke or comment. "No kids up there—unless they're goats..." Or "Bet they wear parachutes to do their yard work up there." Up there. The house was really up there.

The sight of it fired the imagination—terrified people, really. It did not say "Home," it said, "Danger" to most people. It was such a tiny white block, so distant, that people and pets and furniture and household objects of all kinds could be just pouring out the windows—if those were windows—and nobody would be able to tell that things were falling, falling. That was the thing about the house: there was *falling* in your mind when you looked at it. Uncomfortable.

And, of course, everybody wanted to go up there—somehow to get into the good graces of the owner and get up there—just for a look down, and down and down. It's one of the rules: if you are down at the bottom, you look up; if you are up there, you look down. Everyone for miles could see that precarious house, and someone up there could look back. People love to look, and speculate.

***

One of the greatest pig-outs in the county is literally a pig roast which occurs annually in the Parthenon Valley. People from all over the county are invited or come as guests of the invited. A specially-built pit on the site is the center of the party for the first part of the evening, and then the "roasted one" is transported to the starting point of the buffet line, and then the action follows the roast pork as it is placed on the plates, and as it moves along through a gauntlet of pot-luck dishes, drinks, desserts, special treats... Well, you get the picture. The pig is the star of the show, and the action is where the pig is, no matter how piecemeal... Never mind.

But imagine about a hundred guests, semi-dressed-up: grateful for the beauty around them, and the prosperity, and the peace, and the privilege of knowing each other. That's what the roast is about, year after year. In with the fun and the feasting, there is prayer, respect, gratitude.

As the sun goes down and darkness engulfs the valley floor, guests at the pig roast can look up and see, in the last of the sunlight, that little house, looking like a glowing brick at the top of a huge wall: one white brick. And the talk is bound to start up.

Wifey and I, it could be argued, got things going that one year. The long-time locals had processed the phenomenon and dealt with it and were over it. But we, Wifey and I, had to know about such things. (Well, I had to know the story, and Wifey had to know how to get up there!)

"What's that white thing up there—way up there on that mountain?" Wifey innocently asked the Hat Lady, Madge Colstad (her old charity auction buddy), as we sat eating salted-in-the-shell peanuts at a table in the shelter. (The pig was not yet ready, and we were socializing and anticipating and nibbling.)

"That's a house, Deary. And there's quite a story about that," she said, rolling her eyes a little. I always liked Madge. She wore some of the strangest hats in captivity, this night no exception—a huge, autumn festival/war protest/ banana boat thing, with fishing lures. Heart of gold, though. The neighbor lady had moved away, and our source of real big time gossip had dried up. So Wifey was working on Madge.

"Give," said Wifey. She's from Long Island, and up there they don't mess around. They cut to the chase.

"Well," said Madge, her voice getting more raspy as she lowered her tone, "A man built that house up there for a woman, word has it. And then he couldn't find a woman! Certainly not one who would want to live up there where you can spit a thousand feet. The house is vacant."

"He built that for a woman?" said Wifey. And she gave me a look. I don't know why.

"Yep. Then he couldn't find one who would marry him. That's the word."

"Well, that's not the only word," said Ma Wainwright, the ever-present companion and best friend of The Hat Lady. Ma had on a bright yellow sweat suit, as she frequently did when she was "out." And, with her unfortunate and undeserved bulk, she had a school bus look about her. Sort of a nostalgia trip for me. She looked well-tailored that night, and I could see that she had indeed lost some weight. It had been noted in the paper—she was a TOPS champion there for a while a year or two back. And both of us loved Ma Wainwright, make no mistake.

"Really?" said Madge to Ma. "I always heard it was a woman…"

"Oh, there was a woman, all right. The man had the house built up there to win a woman, but when she got up there, she couldn't stand it. Scared the fire out of her. She left. The house is vacant."

This was juicy. We had to find out more about it, so when Wifey and I started drifting around the party, which covered over an acre, searching for the most familiar faces, we asked questions.

Everybody had heard something, but most had to say that they didn't know anything for certain. There were rumors, and there was talk, and there was gossip, and there were stories. It all sounded pretty much the same, no matter how we heard it. We drifted out by the pig roasting in the pit, and a real giggle-box of a lady, small and just all smiles, told us that the man did build the house for a woman who had promised to marry him, but that the woman had backed out at the last minute. The house was vacant. We dismissed that story as too simple.

Moose Vandergrift was at the event, of course, and he was in on removing the pig from the pit and transporting it to the head of the buffet line. He grunted loudly with the strain of it, and I thought I saw flame coming out of his nostrils. Probably an illusion of some sort. Moose had new overalls on—fit for the occasion. I didn't bother him about the mystery house.

While I was "pit-side," I got a good look at the pig, and it was just too late: there was no hope for it. Doc Schullenheimer checked but could not find a pulse. So it goes.

Old Wainwright Himself was there. I did not approach him, though he was unarmed. I saw Rocko, but couldn't get to him, and I had already talked to him about the house up there anyway—at Bingo. He said there were no berries up top there. The brake-job mechanic from the village was on board, and we talked briefly—about brakes. The guy from the feed store was there, and he recalled my pathetic little chain saw with great amusement. We got around and socialized pretty well, now that I think about it.

We found a young fellow, about 45 (just a kid), who had been up there and had actually painted that house. It had been a terrifying experience, and one can of the white paint had gotten away from him and rolled right to the edge of the cliff, and, as far as he knew, it was still there. He had no interest in going after it. He mentioned something about the water supply problem up top there, too. He drifted off before we could get more out of him, but I was encouraged. Someone had actually been up there—had first hand knowledge.

Inside the huge machine shed where the musicians were playing country music, the host had a regular sports shop set up—bows and crossbows and fire arms, and camouflaged everything—right inside the huge shed—a barn, really, but a modern, metal building. And a husky, tough-looking lady in the sports shop told us that the man had built the house up there for a woman, but that she had fallen in love with the house painter and run off with him. The house, she said, was vacant. We believed her and tried in vain to re-locate the house painter. He was simply gone by then.

Our host told Wifey that he had seen lights up there from time to time. "That could have been anything," he said mysteriously.

"Including actual by-god lights," I thought out loud. But I believed him. He lived there. I tried to imagine how his whole layout must look from up there. It was a huge place compared to ours, and it was flat. Someone could be up there watching over the party. I looked up at the cliff at that time, wanting to see some kind of a light, but darkness had engulfed everything. It was time to eat.

A man helping our host cut up the pig said that he could tell us what happened up there at that house, so Wifey and I listened as we piled the roast pork on our plates. "The man built the house for the woman—but it took so long to build it that they both got too old to live up there! The house is vacant." And then I could see that he was just needling our host, who was in the construction business locally. Not a very dependable version, I concluded—just a way of saying that local construction projects took a lot of time sometimes—and up there, forget it!

Dr. Schullenheimer had heard some things, but, in keeping with his professional background, he never repeated stuff like that because he was uncertain of the accuracy, and we understood that, being conscientious non-gossipers ourselves. He did mention that nobody seemed concerned about the place except Wifey and me. (I hate it when fact breaks in.)

We fled Doc's tight-lipped presence and found others to pump for information, rumor, speculation, anything. Some were just not talking—had other interests going. It was like talk about the yellow caution light prospect, the old bottomless pit routine, and a dozen other juicy items that stimulated us—and us only, it seemed. The prayer before the meal had said it all: this bash was about gratitude, prosperity, fellowship, and mutual respect, and good food—not the house up there.

Half-way out of the compound, along the dark driveway, Wifey and I stumbled upon a small group of guests who were drinking—actual alcoholic beverages. They were of no help whatsoever. They were outside of the main party for reasons involving respect: for the host and hostess, for the other guests, and for the occasion itself. What they were doing was not illegal, but it was separate. That happens a lot in our county. There is a tenderness about it. We had a taste of native wine.

But then, back inside near the musicians, I was grabbed by Old Rathbone, who had heard me fishing for rumors.

"Out diggin' around fer some gossip, I see," he said to me, coming at me all self-righteous and bug-eyed. I was innocently trying, at that moment, to listen to the music and eat. I insist.

"I'm here for some *roast* pig," I said, "but you'll do. Good evening."

"You don't want to know the truth about that there house. It ain't fer outsiders like you-uns." Evidently Wifey and I had become obvious in our quest. But Rathbone did not talk to Wifey. Many men in the area shoulder out the women present when they talk to other men.

"I thought you were an outsider yourself, Rathbone."

"Well, I'm gettin' over that. Anyways, best you stay away from that house." He was certainly trying to talk like the perceived local. Imitation hayseed, I thought.

"Why?" asked Wifey.

He had physically turned, pointing himself away from Wifey. "Tell your missus that they's places you go and places you don't go," Rathbone told me. He did not look directly at Wifey, although I saw him glance once—and not at her face.

"That bad, huh?" I said.

"Yep. Bad as it gets. Jist a word to the wise."

Give it to Wifey: she did not attack. It was a party, we were happy to be there, and Rathbone was clueless. I felt Wifey bristle, but she, on her own, stayed the impulse. I think she kicked herself under the table.

Well, of course, Old Rathbone could hardly contain himself.

I didn't like Rathbone anymore because he thought I was both ignorant and stupid—as well as completely beneath him socially and intellectually, but I decided to drop him a cue so that he could tell me what he was just dying to tell me. Then I decided to just let him twist in the wind for a while, and I ate silently. Good pork. Everything good. Wifey not in attack mode. Diet Coke, too! No kicks under the table for me. The best of all possible worlds.

"Well?" said Old Rathbone after a minute or so.

"Well what?"

"Ain't you gonna pick my brain here? As usual, I know somethin' you don't know."

"If this is about my neighbor, I don't want to hear it," I said. He had been all over me about "allowing" someone to build a house too close to our land—said any neighbor that close had to be a relative. I was sick of Old Rathbone.

"This is about that house up there, son. And you and your missus have gotta know about it, right?"

"Oh, go ahead," I said finally, "tell me all about it. I've heard it all anyway. Shoot."

Old Rathbone sort of cleared a circle: created a confidential zone—moving his eyes around as if spies were everywhere. "A man built that house on that there cliff fer a woman. Trouble of it was, neither of them knowed she was a somnambulist. You know what that is, boy?"

"My God. She was a sleepwalker?"

"That's the ticket. They musta learned you somethin' in that trade school you went to and called it an education. Yep, they say she got up in the middle of their weddin' night and walked off that cliff. And the house ain't vacant, it's haunted these days. She's up there, and she ain't happy, and she has been seen. Ain't safe to go there, mark my words." And *then* he looked directly at Wifey.

"So, it's a ghost story now?" I ventured.

"They's lots of ghosts in the county," said Old Rathbone, "and you'd know that if'n you'd pay attention to your betters."

"Get yourself some pork," I said to Rathbone, "unless you're already full—of bull."

"Some folks, " he said, "might wonder why certain other folks have seen a light up there sometimes—of a dark night when it was cold and miserable out. Them that pays attention might wonder." And then he was just through with me—threw up his hands, rolled his eyes, and stomped away in disgust. There was just no hope for the likes of me.

***

Wifey is now working on Rick Roller, our hyperactive friend, to get up there to that house, hiking or on an ATV, or on a dirt bike—somehow. They might parachute in, or scale the cliff. To them, it is irrisistible. I have little to say in the matter. It probably involves a stretch of private road that Roller hasn't traveled, and now that Wifey's running around with an ATV, they're going to the top of that mountain someday, and they will knock on that door, together. If a ghost answers, I refuse to be responsible, and I have said so. I can't do anything about Wifey's penchant for gossip, either. I'll have a nice bowl of chili ready for the adventurers when they come down. If they come down.

Meanwhile, I have a theory or two. I think the man was challenged—perhaps by a woman—to build a house up there. He accepted the challenge and built the house because a man's gotta do what a man's gotta do. Or, maybe he just wanted to build a house right there—maybe he just thought a mistake had been made, and a house simply belonged up there, clinging. In old England, they used to call such things "follies." Of course, I refuse to speculate, and I hate gossip. It's just not in me. I insist.

BURNING DAYLIGHT

I lay on the huge rock at the very bottom of the canyon, beside The Little Mother, The Big Mother, and The Three Sisters—rock barriers in one of the area's premier canoe and kayak rivers, and I was examining a cliff made up of toothy rock "monsters" who seemed to be focusing on some hated object in that wilderness that I could not see. Later, I learned what it was they hated.

Rick Roller had finally succeeded in getting Wifey and me involved in his life. It had become his job to ride every trail, swim every river, plunge over every waterfall, turn over every rock, and poke into every shadow in the county, and today we were in it with him—plummeting down cascades of basketball-sized rocks on an All-Terrain Vehicle (ATV), then climbing back up, almost immediately, fording rivers, dangling our feet over cliffs, hopping around on "skyscraper" rock formations, bounding and bouncing over exposed roots and fallen trees, for miles and miles and miles. I now lay on the rock in a place where few humans have been.

Of course, among those few were the maimed and the deceased, for the rocks in the river, when the river was high and fast, had splattered lots of people like Rick. And me. Bodies, alive and dead, had been winched out of that hole. Untold tons of canoe and kayak wreckage, too. Today the river was low and slow. I liked it.

There are apparently legions of people who must "boldly go where no man has gone..."—who have to see it, climb it, swim it, drive it, fly it, find it, grab it, jump off it, jump over it, or whatever is indicated, whatever it is. Me? I had been riding along all afternoon like a sack of feed on Wifey's ATV, a passenger. I had been transported to one of Nature's rare and wonderful creations, and the nightmare of the journey was simply the price of the dream. You've gotta get there somehow, apparently, or you are not alive.

**

"Come on, we're burning daylight," The Leader had said. And we mounted up and lunged forward into the abyss, Wifey at the controls because of her 20 years of experience with motorcycles. And I was behind her all the way (well, above, behind, around, beside, upon—all prepositions and positions apply), sitting in a Wal-Mart boat seat precariously lashed to the rear cargo rack with Velcro straps. It was like riding an epileptic bronco during an earthquake/avalanche/volcanic eruption. It was not what the manufacturers envisioned, according to the manual, and the law. But, of course, we were out "playing."

All over those rigs there are stickers and signs: **Do not ride double. Do not carry passengers, you fool. Do not operate vehicle on public roads and highways except in an emergency. Wear a helmet at all times. This means you, you dipstick.** And other signs could have adorned our vehicle: **Do not go up the faces of cliffs. Do not go off cliffs. Do not plunge into raging rivers, race with maniacs at 50 miles per hour, dive into bottomless pits, hit small trees. In short, don't follow that crazy S.O.B.**

But Rick had a passenger, too—a friend of his wife. She kept taking pictures and writing down notes, obviously wanting to treasure the moments forever. Forever, I observed, is relative. She was lighter than I, so she was not as good at making the front end of the vehicle jump up in the air, threatening to dump the whole thing over backwards. Lightweight. And she was accustomed to "leaning," apparently—a regular expert.

"Look at his eyes," I warned her as we zoomed down a rural dirt road at about forty miles per hour, side-by-side. "Look at his eyes!" Rick looked like Hitler announcing the invasion of Poland. He looked like Dr. Frankenstein about to turn on the juice. He looked like Ahab riding the white whale. He looked like any bug-eyed, raving lunatic in any B-grade horror movie I'd ever seen. The women howled with laughter as we pitched and careened. Once, when Wifey's head turned around completely backwards—or seemed to—I saw the same look in her eyes. Madness is communicable. Go figure.

"Send help," I yelled at a load of hunters we streaked by at the edge of the wilderness, but I don't know where they would have sent the help. One rock pile is as good as another, I suppose. We plunged into the heart of darkness, and I understood Joseph Conrad quite well. Nature is capable of reclaiming us: of muting the voices of our education, of laying bare our primitive aspects, of filtering out our common sense. Soon we were miles out of reach of any help.

The desperately disturbed do not understand the rest of us. They will tolerate us, but they do not comprehend self-preservation instincts, yearnings for security and comfort, or the desire not to spend Forever in a body cast. It is beyond them. Time spent on hesitation and caution is termed "burning daylight." I could tell that these people were all desperately disturbed. I was alone.

For hours, we lurched through one jagged morass after another, tumbling, jerking, wrenching, connected to the ground by whichever wheel was willing. My friends were taking me out to view Nature's wonders. We were going for the gusto. This was fun. They insisted. I hung on, trying to make sense of the topography, just in case I survived the inevitable and had to drag the corpses of the rest of them out of there.

High in the sky, I could occasionally see con trails. Six or eight miles away, there were other human beings—straight up there. I tried to signal with my glasses, but they were too dirty.

"Where are we, Rick?" I would challenge, as we plunged into a river, tossing and churning.

"We're right here," he would say. And I would look around, and, of course, it was true: I could see all of them and they could see me. We were all there together, in over our heads. Loony laughter all around.

"How long have we been lost?" I asked once—just out of curiosity.

"All day long," Rick Roller said. "Ain't that neat?" And then we would skirt a huge mud puddle, whip around a curve, leap over a fallen tree, and dive down a boulder-strewn chute, Wifey screaming from the thrill of it all. She rode a helluva race! I was proud of her. That's my woman!

We climbed Satan's Ladder, edged along Dumbo's Tightrope, inched our way around Suicide Loop and Hell's Hairpin, and slalomed down Avalanche Alley; then we did the tough stuff. Sometimes I rode, sometimes I pushed, sometimes I just flew.

"Don't try this at home, Kids," Rick would say, and the debris would fly in all directions as he found a more difficult route, motor revving, women screaming and giggling.

The ATV had a rugged motor, and it would do wonderful things—perform feats of balance and strength I hadn't thought possible. You don't get to see Bambi and Thumper while you are out there, though: they hear you coming and try to get a good, safe seat for when you wipe out and go splat (the train-wreck syndrome). I saw one ground squirrel all day, and when I asked it to call 911, it just looked at me.

"Lean!" yelled the woman clinging to Rick's back, "Lean!" Somehow, as I was hanging on by the fingernails and expecting to be tossed over the brink of a cliff at any moment, I was supposed to lean—lean into the hill and quit acting like a sack of feed. Lean, and quit flopping around like a boneless pulp. Lean, and quit screaming. Lean left, lean right, lean forward.

"You lean," I yelled back. "I'm trying to stay on this hoss. " (They all said I was just being stubborn. I was being sane. Sanity is misunderstood today.) The woman slapped me on the back at that point, to "encourage" me. A mushroom shaped cloud rose from my filthy shirt, a very menacing development, but nobody seemed surprised.

***

I was over the denial phase, the deal-making phase, and the prayer phase as I lay on that rock down there at the bottom of everything. Of course, I could not risk shutting my eyes. I was at peace and probably looked restful, except for the twitching and a few spasms. Even corpses do that. I had not given up, either: it had all been confirmed, as far as I was concerned. I was alive. God was up there somewhere. This rock was an answered prayer. It was solid, firm, safe. It was my island: sanctuary, respite, sanity.

Wifey was in the water. It was late October, and Wifey and the other lady were in the water—the ice water—Wifey with her clothes and boots on. I was afraid to look very closely at the other woman. I learned her name, though: Ilene. Of course. It didn't matter much, though. She was doomed. They both were.

The rock was fine for me, warm and dry and mentally stimulating. Right away I was stimulated to think about how to get up out of there. According to my calculations, we would have only about fifty miles of hell-bent riding, straight uphill and through uncharted forests, to get to safety. Probably the women would freeze to death, and then Rick and I would thaw, cook, and eat them, boots and all. Weeks later, our remains would be found by hunters beside an SOS we had tramped out in the snow. The dead ATVs, with their empty gas tanks and smooth tires, would be extracted by ecologists. My manuscripts would be salvaged from my "Documents" by my son the computer whiz. They would want Rick's brain for science. Others would penetrate the wilderness on ATVs and search for mementos, bones, and debris. There would be stories, legends! You see things clearly while you are lying on an island rock in the wilderness.

"Come on! We're burning daylight," a voice broke in. It was Wifey's voice this time. She had mutated completely. I left the sanctity of my rock and mounted up behind her on the infernal machine. She was cold and clammy, but gung-ho.

It had taken hours of pell-mell pitching and plummeting to get down to those rocks, but when we mounted up again and headed up the nearest craggy flume, we were on decent road within half an hour. (I was, by then, willing to call anything short of a cluster-bombing a "decent road.") Daylight was fading.

I eyed Rick Roller with new suspicion. He and Wifey and Ilene had been passing secret signals, I had noticed—wry little smiles and winks. (I have an instinct about these things.) There had obviously been an easier way into that beautiful, inaccessible gulch. We had taken a circuitous route just for the recreation. Wifey had needed practice with suicidal vertical maneuvering. Rick had provided the opportunity. We had been "playing." "I have learned to play," Wifey was saying. "I have learned to play." Go figure.

In the world of ATV zealots, we had done the "purist" thing: extreme riding. "Smooth" is not in their vocabulary. Survival is not a priority. Adrenalin is their drug of choice. (Those people practice their maniacal grins in the mirror in their lairs at night. Rick Roller is probably their role model and demon king.)

Soon we were on public roads and even highways. It was all legal now, of course, because, as far as I was concerned, this was an emergency. The only shaking on our rig was Wifey's shivering. If the police stopped us, I would take over and argue that these insane people were *rescuing* me, and it was an emergency situation and these were emergency vehicles. And it was getting dark. I was sure I could display an array of bruises. If that didn't work, I could argue that *I* was rescuing *them* and getting them the help and the cages they needed. But, alas, no police found us.

***

At sunset, all of us were safe, alive and well, and munching Wal-Mart trail mix at a scenic overlook frequented by the region's Flying Saucer buffs. Hosts of people had seen fireballs and lights and other UFOs from this roadside vantage point, out there overlooking our wilderness area. "Crazy people," Rick said. "They call 'em The Dover Lights. Weird people." And he got that mad look in his eyes.

Rick had tried to tell a few of the "seekers" that the mysterious lights they were seeing were the campfires of lost ATV riders in the wilderness below—(for we could see miles and miles of it from there). That sounded like a sane explanation to me. Sanity—from Rick Roller's lips. Boggles the mind.

The whole area we had covered lay before us. All of it suddenly made sense. I could see where we had been, where we had ridden (safely, after all), where the girls had gotten wet and horribly cold. With Rick's zoom lens, I could even see the healing rock where I had lain and meditated. And I could see the "monsters" of the cliff, looking right at *us*!

***

Rick claimed that he had in the recent past encountered people with guns chasing UFOs at this spot. "They come roaring up here in a pick-up, drunk, and jump out with their assault rifles, and wait for UFOs to come around the mountain there."

"Ever get picked up by one, Rick?" I asked, innocently popping some trail mix, "A UFO, I mean?"

"Sure," he said, "but you know, they just will not come *back* for me." And he got that daft gaze going, and he laughed like a fiend.

"Phone home, you crazy S.O.B.," I said, "Phone home." I was tired and sore, and impatient—and very grateful that the day was over.

The sun went down then, and we were through burning daylight, I was certain. My deliverance was at hand, most likely. We were going home now. Amen. It was over: my ordeal was over. Probably.

***

We mounted up, and Wifey and Rick started the valiant ATV motors. Then, on one of their snide, secret signals, they both reached down and flipped on the headlights! Those damned things have headlights! The "Playing" was not over. We screamed away into the night, laughing and lurching—and leaning.

AGES AND STAGES

Old Rathbone was one of several "helpful" people in my new life who felt obliged to scold me: to just jump astride me somewhere and flog me senseless with admonitions. Double-Dog Darrell, my corrupting mentor, delighted in it—trying to turn me into a liberal Sixties throw-back, especially when I resisted. The neighbor lady, who at last report was utterly miserable—relocated and unhappy in her new life among the tumbleweeds of the Golden West—always felt duty-bound to inform me of my tastelessness and my hard-headedness when I refused to play the game. She was gone, though. Wifey was still around, however, and she felt that she had a license to kill, when it came to scolding me about my perceived shortcomings. Total strangers seemed ready and willing—eager, even!—to walk up to me occasionally and take their best shot. But Old Rathbone was relentless.

One day, just as I was making inroads into deciding whether to get with the program and be old or go on being precariously young, Old Rathbone swooped down on me like a chicken hawk and pinned me to the swing on the front porch of the Senior Center. I was meditating, profoundly, when I felt his talons.

"Son, you gotta wake up and smell the Geritol."

"Whaaat?"

"You got to realize yerself! You are gettin' old. Face it, Boy. You are mortal."

Well, charming. I really needed to hear that. "And to what do I owe this pithy, if unsolicited, assessment?" I said.

"I'm jist fillin' you in. You ain't bulletproof." He stroked his long white beard and squinted with one eye—a new thing he was trying, I guess.

"Is this about Wifey running me all over the hills on that ATV?" Wifey and I had been AWOL lately because of our new toy. I blamed Rick Roller. He had created a 4-wheeling monster, and now I had to ride with it. We went everywhere.

"No. Boy, you got to git yer flu shot—and take yer vitamins, and quit drinkin' that swill."

"I don't drink," I said firmly.

"Diet Coke. It'll dissolve a nail, you know. What's it doin' to your stomach? And flu season is comin'. Get the shot! And you got to eat vegetables, go to church, be careful, and don't take no chances."

"All that."

"Yep. They's some things you jist got to accept."

"Well," I said desperately, "I fasten my seat belts."

"That ain't enough. You got to slow down—not jist in the car. You ain't as sharp as you used to be, and you probably never was." This from a bald guy with a bandana, a long pointed beard, jeans and engineer boots, and a limp. And tattoos!

"Thank you for that. I was feeling needlessly good there for a while. I apologize."

"Over-confidence. You got to figure that your reflexes ain't as quick as they was, and you ain't as strong or as tough as you was, either—and yer getting' soft and flabby."

"Hey, I work hard—climb mountains—hike trails—ride an ATV—swim the rivers..."

"I'm not talkin' 'bout all that stuff yer wife drags you into. You got to find yerself a rockin' chair, Son, and put some miles on it. You ain't no spring chicken."

"Well, certainly not a rooster, I guess."

"Want to get to sleep at night? Jist start countin' all the things you can no longer do."

"I like to be positive when I can."

"Well, count up all the things you're *positive* you cain't do no more!"

"Well, most of those things I probably never could do—and I'm not sure I remember which is which!"

"See there: that's positive! You might end up thinkin' you did all kinds of good stuff. When you're half asleep, they'll be like memories."

"You're a confusing man, Rathbone. You want me to wake up and smell things, then you tell me to count things to get to sleep."

"You're jist not listenin' to me, Boy."

"Look, what brought all this on?"

"You got old!—that's what brought it on. Don't you know nothin'?"

"What I mean is, why do you think it is your duty to tell me this? Aging I can handle. You, I'm not sure about."

"You been gettin' cocky. You've got some gray hair, you know. And still, you pick up sacks of cement here and there, run around layin' rock, buildin' things—runnin' up and down hills. You got to act yer age!"

"Oh, so I should just throw down and quit and sit on the porch."

"And take it easy," confirmed Old Rathbone, and we both kicked back in the swing.

This was not what had been going on in my world, as far as I was concerned. I was dancing as fast as I could, feeling myself slow down a bit, but plugging away. Folks at the Senior Center were being encouraged to stay active, get with the program, keep moving. What was Rathbone talking about?

"Rathbone, they're down here at the 'Center every day trying to get people to exercise, eat right, get into a hobby or craft, and keep their heads in the game. Why should I slow down?"

"That's fer later," he snarled, waving his arms. He was passioned-up about this for some reason.

"Later? I know you're going to explain this, so go ahead. Flail away."

"See, they's steps and stages and phases that you go through. Now, you got to keep up appearances, and you got to be right, or the villagers will come after you."

"You're kidding me." (I had visions of peasants with pitchforks coming to do me in. I certainly wanted no part of committing a faux pas.)

"Listen, Boy. You are at the stage where you got to accept bein' old. Next, yer gonna hit the stage where you try to act young—but if you act like yer young right now, yer gonna make the old folks mad at you fer showin' off. See what I mean?"

"I can't act like I feel right now, but I can later?"

"That's right if it feels right. Right now, yer in the last stage of bein' younger than the *old* old, so you gotta take it easy and *act* a little bit older. But pretty soon, yer gonna be old—just plain old. THEN you act like yer younger than you are, and everybody will think it's cute."

"Cute."

"Yeah. They'll admire you fer yer spunk. You'll be performin' above and beyond the call of duty. Those are the folks the 'Center is tryin' to get exercisin' and all. Right now, when you wave a leg in the air, they say yer jist rubbin' it in; later, when you wave that same leg, they will say, 'My God—he's seventy, and he can wave his leg in the air. Isn't that great?' See what I mean?"

"Vaguely."

"Right now, if you lose some weight, they'll sneer at you because yer lordin' it over them; when yer seventy and you lose weight, they'll think yer sick."

"So, no weight loss at all, huh?"

"Too risky. Best stay pretty much the way you are—fer your own health. Don't get fat now. Someone will think yer lettin' yerself go—and that's bad. Later on, when you pick up a few pounds, they'll say you look good. You may even get called Jolly and Cute."

"And people sit around and think about this?"

"They do."

"So, maybe if I had a little stroke here—or some kind of a collapse, mysterious and unexplained—I could be more acceptable?"

"Could be you'd get *concern* rather than resentment," Rathbone ventured.

"Concern is good," I said. "I could live with concern. But not pity."

"Then there's yer sex life," Rathbone growled. "Have you noticed anything lately?"

Well, I had to think about that for a minute. But no, I hadn't noticed anything about sex. I had a few distant memories, of course, but the term "sex life" didn't ring any bells.

"That's 'cuz yer *harmless* now, Son. When yuh go to Silver Dollar City and the pretty girls come out into the audience to get a man to get up on stage and make a fool outa himself, who do they grab?"

"They never get me."

"They soon will, though. Only yer wife knows yer harmless now. But word gets out. If yuh got no hair, and yuh look a little long of tooth, or yer a little fat and gray, they jump right on yer lap! 'Cuz yer harmless! The waitresses in the big city the cafés: ever see them rub all over a young man? No. They find a harmless old coot, and show him some cleavage, and run their fingers through his hair. Because he's harmless! He ain't a threat to them in no way." Old Rathbone, with his bald head and his long white beard, looked harmless to me. Maybe he knew something I didn't after all.

"Well, I haven't had anyone on my lap yet. Not up here."

"Well, she's comin'—and when she does it, you'll know that you are no longer a threat to womankind. You are gelded— neutered—harmless! She'll start teasin' you about how handsome you are and how she wants to run off with you. That jist means yer no longer that stud muffin you used to be."

"So, what if I just grab her?"

"Then yer a Dirty Old Man. So you don't grab nobody. End up in jail. Trick is, don't let her know yer age. Always be deceptive."

"Speed up, slow down, act old, act young, be harmless, don't gain, don't lose. I gotta tell yuh, Rathbone, it sounds like a snake pit to me. Are you sure there's no way I can just slog along and age gracefully—sorta one day at a time, with a cumulative effect?"

"Nope. Trust me, son: this is the way it is done."

"I can't just be the way I am?"

"Lord no! You got to *act*—present yourself as this or that, accordin' to what is right for whoever is lookin'."

"And who makes up these rules? Is there a committee somewhere—a council, a think tank?"

"Them's jist the rules, that's all. Be advised."

"I'm going home in a few minutes, Rathbone, and I'm going to worry. Later this afternoon."

"Good."

I went silent for a while, and I stared dramatically into space, thinking about what Rathbone was saying—casting myself and my friends and acquaintances at the 'Center in the main roles. And there was some truth to what he said. "They" seemed to want us to slow down, until age slowed us down, and then they seemed to encourage involvement, exercise, and a speed-up. At sixty, they told us to act our age, be careful, take no chances, and not break a hip or something terrible; at seventy, they wanted people on the treadmill or sitting around waving their arms, lifting weights—or line dancing! "You're never too old..." They would brag about "active Senior Citizens," hold Senior Olympic Games, etc. Timing, it seemed, was terribly important.

"Rathbone, I'm glad we have had this little talk. I was feeling mindlessly secure and comfortable there for a while, and now I'm miserable and worried. I feel like Adam after the forbidden fruit routine. Thank you."

"Someone had to tell you, Son. No trouble at all. And sometime we got to get into this wimp thing you got goin', Son. You let folks run all over you."

"Really? That's what Wifey says."

"Yep. Now I don't know, but maybe God just made you a sheep. But sometimes I think he made you a masochistic sheep to boot!"

"Sort of like a mutton for punishment, huh?"

"Yep. You got to work on that, too." He didn't even laugh.

***

I got off the porch swing, carefully, of course, and some ladies came out of the 'Center, and I suddenly could not move. I could not decide how to move: whether to put a spring in my step and celebrate the last vestiges of my youth, or to grab my hip and limp away, *acting* my age. Or just cower like a whipped pup.

"Hello, ladies. Wonderful day, isn't it!" I ventured, just holding still.

The ladies looked at me, then at Rathbone, and then back at me. "Stay away from that old goat," one of the ladies said loudly, nodding toward Rathbone. "He's so full of it, it's comin' out his ears."

I trotted out to the car, hopped in, and left a little rubber there in the Senior Center parking lot. Then I zoomed off up the mountain. After a couple of curves, sanity prevailed, and I slowed down just a bit. Up by the dump, at the base of Round Top Mountain, I considered pulling off the highway and letting some younger drivers past me. But then I just sneered and dropped the hammer! I was going 40 when I reached Scenic Point. Harmless indeed!

THE SECRET OF LIFE

It is known among locals of a certain strain that marital advice and secret lore about womankind is available at midnight during thunderstorms at the top platform of the tower at Scenic Point. Double-Dog Darrell is there for the believers, with his four wolves, his crow, his eye patch, and his enigmatic face. You must go there, however, face the storm, make the climb, and believe.

On the night of a full moon, preferably at midnight, general wisdom based on collected poetic passages and Darrell's detailed local travel is there for the seeker of truth. Often a flowing cape is part of the guru's costume for such occasions. The crow always sits on his right shoulder; the wolves always face the East, the West, the North, and the South; sometimes there are hors d'oeuvres. Usually, tourists do not attend those midnight sessions..

Often, on a bright sunny morning up top—when there is low fog down on the river and the valley looks like a feathery ocean from the tower—very deep philosophy, set forth in crisp and pithy rhetoric, is flung out there for those who already have wisdom enough to listen. It's an iffy situation, and a lot depends on Double-Dog's health situation, his general mood, and the dominance of a given personality from his considerable quiver of personalities. Tourist curiosity/participation is critical also.

It is rumored that, if you can make the scene at 4 a.m. on Lawrence Welk's birthday during National Dental Hygienist's Week and Take Your Lemur to Work Day, Double-Dog Darrell will answer your most terrible questions, change your life, validate your parking, and send you away a completely new person—with a handsome tote bag and some complementary personal care items. That is just an elaborate rumor.

My problem was always the same: my time was not my own, and I could not get there when I wanted to be there. It was only blind luck, usually, when I climbed the tower for a visit. Berries, Bingo, Bowling, and Branson had me on a treadmill; the Senior Citizens' Center, pool, Wifey's ATV riding, building, breaking, and re-building at the house—all of it had me running in circles. It was making me old.

Or something was.

In desperation, I simply reached out and ripped a day right out of the calendar, and I took it for myself, my soul, my mind, my heart. (Dramatic, huh?) I drove alone to Scenic Point on the day after Thanksgiving, and I climbed the tower. It was a gray, cold, miserable day.

***

The great shoppers were off to Harrison, Russellville, Branson, Eureka Springs, Fayetteville, or even Springfield for a day of tenacious power shopping; the great hermits and ascetics were out in the woods—"far from the madding crowd"; Double-Dog Darrell, I assumed, would be up there at the top of the tower, ready for action.

I was beyond the reach of ordinary wisdom. I knew the good stuff: that each day is a gift, that I am involved in mankind but that to view mankind I must withdraw to a respectful distance, that Faith is salvation and a telescope, that beauty is truth and truth is beauty, that Nature never did betray the heart that loved Her, that marriage is a oneness, divine and indivisible, that men and women often interpret each other's reactions as actions, and that a wet bird does not fly by night. All the good stuff. My concern that day was with Time: its quantity, its quality, and its velocity.

But I could sense at the bottom of the frosty steps of the tower that something was different. There had been a disturbance in The Force. It was like when you approach a room and you just know it is empty before you look inside or enter. Something was missing—not right—out of whack.

Well, for one thing, the horse was not there. Double-Dog's car was there, the only one in the county that was older than mine (without being a designated antique vehicle). Then I had a feeling there were not enough wolves for a quorum. As I approached the top steps of the tower, I could tell that I was right: only two wolves. And no crow at all! Darrell wore the flowing cape, but the rest of his outfit was not tourist-baiting grade, and he had on his blue eye patch, which is simply not as menacing as the black one. The man actually had on a stocking cap and a London Fog topcoat! Go figure. Double-Dog Darrell was barely on duty.

Scenic Point is reputed to be an ancient power source with great magic and "big medicine" in Indian lore, and it is obviously a place where even the most casual tourist can stop and re-charge: energize, if you will. I use it for that, and other denizens of the area do, too, whether or not they admit it. Easter Sunrise services are held there; individuals and groups go there for prayer and meditation; it is a pivot point, a juncture, a rendezvous for mystical beings. It is high ground and a place for pausing to make adjustments and to contemplate the recent climb, the impending descent. I insist. (They've also got a coke machine there.) What I needed that day was the sheer voltage of the place.

"Are you sick?" I asked. Double-Dog looked like something just thrown together—or dragged through a knot hole. He had a harried look. He was out of sync.

"Yes, I am sick, but I am not ill," he said. "A boulder has fallen, just downhill there a little. A reminder."

"I saw," I told him. "It's a big one. Someone could have been hurt." Right by the highway a hundred yards down there was a new boulder, freshly tossed down by the mountain.

"Have you thought about its meaning?" asked the guru.

"Yeah. Chance intervened, and nobody was hurt. The rock landed. Works for me."

"Wrong. Its meaning is all wrapped up in why you have come here today."

"You know why I have come?"

"Certainly. I have instincts and powers—intuition and insight, beyond the comprehension of mortal men."

"You talked to my wife, didn't you."

"Yeah. She said you were bummed out about gettin' old. I knew you would come here. Again. Still."

I could tell he had just grabbed some clothes and headed for the tower—that this was not a full-blown session at all. This was just a patched-together deal. I was concerned. The session might not "take."

"I think we need to do something about Time," I said.

"The boulder fell. The mountain is dissolving. Time is on the march. It should remind you that there is an alternative to growing old. But nobody was flattened by this boulder. It was a free one." And Double-Dog sneezed.

"A free one? What does that mean? Perhaps I have you at a bad time." (I would have said "God Bless you," but DDD already knew about that.)

"What kind of time is bad time? Time is what has you concerned. There is no bad time. Carpe Diem!"

"Okay, but there's a trap in all that. If I indeed 'seize the day' and fill each moment with activities—fun and games, study and music and art, sport and spiritual pursuits, and all of that—Time absolutely flies! Poof! It is gone. If I don't go for the gusto, I get bored—and Time goes slower, but I feel wasteful."

"Bingo," he said enigmatically, pointing his finger at me. I had obviously said something wise and true, and I was proud; still, I was confused.

"And exercise: Exercise is supposed to gain me some time, right?—make my body last longer. But exercise seems wasteful when there is work to be done! And I get competitive when I exercise, and I end up sore, it hurts, and I feel old—and it lasts a long time. And the more I do, the more I *can* do, and there is no end to it. I would rather do beneficial work."

"Bingo," said Double-Dog Darrell triumphantly. I knew I had said something significant this time. He got that thousand-yard stare going—the look school teachers and administrators master, where they are aware not only of the person in front of them, but also of things going on all around the room or down the hallway or across the field. I knew that trick myself.

"I try to 'push the envelope,' as the cliché goes, but sooner or later I reach my limitations (with pool, bowling, ATV riding, hiking, sketching, whatever), and that doesn't feel good. I don't want to *know* my limits! Suspicion is enough. I just feel that Time has already clobbered me."

"Bingo!" he said again, coughing. Probably his word for being clobbered, right? A boulder fell—Bingo! I had another birthday—Bingo! Time was kicking my butt—Bingo! My hair turned gray—Bingo! I lost my car keys in my own pocket—Bingo! I needed his help, and, Bingo, I was being dismissed.

And that just about did it for me. I was about ready to go back down to the parking lot and leave the babbling numbskull to his miseries. I didn't need any obscurist puzzles. If you're gonna be a weird mystic seer on a frozen mountaintop, you should give 100%, right?

"Bingo. I climb all the way up here and tell you what's eating me, and all you can say is Bingo? I think you're having a really bad day—one of your worst—and I am further wasting my precious Time here."

"On my worst day," said Double-Dog Darrell, wiping his nose, "and this may well be one of my worst, I am certainly not wastin' the precious time of the likes of you. If you are incapable of recognizin' encapsulated genius, it is not my fault. *You* are wastin' *my* time. You have presented me with questions. My answer is quite simple. Bingo."

"Yeah, right."

The only Bingo that I knew about was Thursday night with Rocko and the bunch at the Legion Hall, and I just knew that it had nothing to do with my disagreements with Father Time. I was convinced that Double-Dog Darrell had finally missed one dosage too many and was no longer a dependable sorcerer/witch doctor/oracle/soothsayer/wizard.

"Thank you," I said wryly, "for your time. I had thought you would have suggestions about how to slow the leakage of Time from my life, how to remove the pain of it. But I see that you are otherwise occupied. I'd like to recommend some little green capsules from Wal-Mart. Fix you right up." And I started down the steps, a disillusioned, disappointed pilgrim. Stocking cap, London Fog topcoat—not the uniform of an oracle. He was just phoning it in!

"All right, all right, I'll spell it out for you," he said, stopping me. "But you gotta work with me here."

"Please proceed," I said, returning to the top platform. (Yeah: a snit. Beneath me, I know.)

"Bingo, it could be argued, is the perfect activity. It makes physical strength irrelevant. It makes intelligence and skill irrelevant, too. It is not painful, not personal, not your fault—or anybody's. The numbers pour out of the hopper completely at random, and you either have them on your cards or you don't. If you are six or sixty, you either have the number or you don't. Youth is irrelevant. Age means nothing. You don't exert, you don't strain, you don't get sore, you don't tax your brain, you barely have to be awake. If you can't hear, you can see the numbers on the wall. If you miss a session, you can say you would have won had you been there, and nobody could argue much. Bingo is social; it's slow and low impact; it gets you out of the house; you don't have to dress up, and you can go to the john between games. The proceeds go to a good cause."

"All true, but Bingo is hardly the secret of life."

"I'm not so sure. Each time a number pops out of the hopper, there is hope, anticipation. Every time! That is a lot of hope, concentrated. Everybody *almost* wins. Nobody wins every game. There is always hope for everybody in the next game. Hope springs eternal! It is not evil—not gambling: a churchy decision has been made. And there is choice: you don't have to play. There is risk, but you don't have to risk—you have a choice. But really, all you have to do is show up."

"I suppose *watching* Bingo would probably be better," I said thoughtfully.

"That," said Darrell, "would slow Time down better than anything I can think of. Well, maybe watching curling or auto racing on TV…"

I knew that I had to stop Double-Dog right there or he would get into the numerology aspect of the game and I would be completely snowed. All those numbers, and the combinations… mind boggling. And I needed to be polite, even grateful, and I needed to behave as if I understood, and agreed. And Double-Dog didn't look well; I think the flu was getting him. Him!

"You know," I said, "you can eat and drink while playing Bingo—or talk on the phone, now that I think about it. I suppose you could exercise—or work. You could play Bingo even if you had a cold—or the flu. When I was a teacher, I would have graded papers while playing…"

"See what I mean? Perfect. You could cook, drive a car, write poetry, paint pictures, almost anything—and the numbers and the hope would still roll out of that hopper, and it would be all good!"

"So, what's the grabber?" I said, knowing full well that there was a grabber because there always is.

DDD adjusted his blue eye patch, straightened, and regarded the eastern horizon. A gust of harsh cold wind hit us hard, right there at the good moment. "In Bingo, as in all of life, you have to deal with whatever pops out of the hopper. That's the grabber. Those are the rules." Then he sneezed and brought up his handkerchief again.

"I can work with that," I told him. And I had to admire him. He had worked through the pain—functioned, though caught off balance. "Not bad for an off day. You have done well."

And then Double-Dog Darrell removed his eye patch and extended his hand to me. "Thank you," he said. "I haven't been any of my selves lately, and you have anchored me." Double-Dog's personality wasn't just split, it was julienned! London Fog! Indeed.

"Good," I said. "But one more thing: that free square in the middle of the card—always you get a free square. Bothersome, don't you think?"

"Ah, the free square in the center: most fascinating. A whole chapter. No time today. But I suppose we can think of the boulder, right? It was a free one, too. Sometimes we get a free one."

Right there at the end, too. The fallen boulder and the center square—all tied up together somehow. Cryptic stuff! Go figure.

And we ended the meeting there. I was exhausted anyway, and Double-Dog needed to get horizontal in some warm place, soon. I saw him weeks later, though, and he was fine.

***

I am better now, too, but I have troubling questions about this Bingo business. I may have to go into that with Double-Dog Darrell during the next thunderstorm. Why is Wifey kicking my butt at Bingo every Thursday night? And, if it is all chance, why her? Why not me? And why *is* the center square free? (Sometimes the center square is all I get.) And the very image of Double-Dog playing Bingo—even knowing about Bingo—keeps me awake some nights. Not all, but some.

Life is good, but life is complex.

MY EARWORM

E arworm" is the name that has been given to the affliction of having a tune stuck in one's head. Everything has to have a name, I guess.

As Wifey and I roamed the back roads of the county on our new ATV, my brain was assailed by "Dueling Banjos," the background music of *Deliverance*, a movie that gave fair warning to city folks about intruding on country life. I had my suspicions about just how welcome we were in the real boonies. As we sped up or slowed down, that guitar/banjo theme kept pace, re-playing and echoing—bouncing off canyon walls, having "breakdowns" on rocky cascades, slowing almost to a stop as we approached strangers for directions. I had earworm, and I had it bad. And we were perpetually lost, way out there in the hills.

***

Operators of tourist-contact establishments knew the difficulties better than most. Someone from Chicago would be trying to find a bed and breakfast, a cabin, a rural church or graveyard, and a gas station or gift shop would be the place to ask directions. Maps would come out, and then the fun would begin.

"This road is now a trail. The map hasn't been updated. You can't get there in your car. And this road is not numbered, but it's off to your left down this way on Highway Seven by the log cabin with the morning glories. Are you from around here? It's the old Gibson place, but they've put in a bridge now and it looks different…"

Very often, rather than struggling with such directions, the helpful local would just say, "Tell you what: follow me." And the seeker would be taken to a spot where final, specific directions could be given.

"All right, this is The Cliff House. Go back toward Jasper and take the first right. Look sharp. It's hard to see. And Hang on, because you're going straight down." We both gave and received such directions.

Wifey, it turned out, had no objection to running around utterly lost for hours and hours, with me strapped to the back end of the ATV with my earworm. The county's dirt roads were not marked with names or numbers at all. I, of course, jumped to the conclusion that this was because all of our tax money had been sent to Iraq to coax people who had been killing each other for 4000 years to love each other instantly (and shuck us some oil.) Old Rathbone, however, had informed me that the roads had all been numbered and labeled at one time, but that mysterious locals in the hinterlands had shot them to pieces, ripped them out, or run them down. I was skeptical. We procured maps, and, sure enough, all the roads shown had numbers. There were no corresponding numbers on the roads themselves, though. No signs. No clues. Many roads were not shown, and many that were shown did not turn out to be exactly roads. And Wifey loved it. Wifey had been out there with a kindred spirit, ATV maniac Rick Roller, and those people are not like the rest of us at all: they thrive on uncertainty and insecurity.

But when Wifey and I stopped to ask for directions, things got complicated. "Go down here about two mile to where the old schoolhouse foundation used to be before they bulldozed it. And turn left on that road that goes about straight up. Don't go right. Nobody comes back from there. I think they's a red ribbon a-hangin' on a tree there now. Then, when you git to the dead end, slip around to the side of the big rock and take the loggin' road about five mile down to where that old pond was before they drained it a-lookin' fer bodies... Tell you what: follow me." Nice folks, but perplexed. Not their fault.

No numbers. "Go down 16 to 23 and turn right and go two miles," would have been helpful. The map would say 58, but a brownish signpost would say 1102 to indicate the very same road, and then we would pop up in someone's yard—with dogs barking and curtains moving at the windows. Or the road would file off to a point and disappear in the trees or run into a cliff or a river, or down into the ground. Certainly there had to be some secret method, right?

Wifey was fearless. "Sir, is this a driveway or a road?" she would ask some armed person out in the woods—as the banjo rang in my ears.

"This is *my* road," would often be the answer. And I would search the thicket around the perimeter for gun muzzles, crossbows, overalls, with a banjo "Ringa-ding-*ding* ding" screaming at me, and a guitar answering from the shadows!

Ridiculous, of course. There is no record of people having been killed and eaten by residents of the deep woods of our county. Of course, there is no record of the road past their house, either. There are stupid legends and myths, I hope. When the map-maker gives up on the road, and the road becomes an uncharted ATV trail, and then all of it is washed out and turns into a stony chute, you have a right to some banjo music in your brain, the way I see it.

***

We were out past Acropolis one day, going up the road designated 75B on a hand-drawn map Wifey and Rick Roller stole from a drunken biker at a pie supper, and we pulled into the driveway of the Elkwing Church, just to catch our breath. One of the county workers was there with an unidentifiable (to us) piece of heavy equipment—probably a blackberry shredder, now that I think about it. Of course, we were lost.

"Excuse me," said Wifey to the man. "Can you tell us where this road leads?"

"The road goes anywhere you want it to," said the man.

Well, that was helpful. But what that meant, we supposed, was that it would come out somewhere and someone there would know where the hell we were—and from there we could go anywhere: to safety, perhaps, or perhaps to our doom. Or Swain or Nail.

As we talked and probed for details, we got out our other

map—one Wifey got from the county judge himself. It was all quite confusing to the county worker who worked on instinct and previous experience and knew perfectly well where he was.

Presently, another ATV approached us from back of the church. My earworm absolutely jangled! The guy did not look friendly. In six years in the hills, I had not seen a face like that. The eyes were dead eyes; the smile included a sneer. He looked meaner than my friend Rocko in a supposedly secret berry patch. He was wearing overalls, like my overalls, and like those of the throw-backs in *Deliverance*. I wanted Wifey to hit the road and go somewhere, anywhere—which was, after all, where the road went. But not Wifey.

"Sir," she said as the fellow shut off his motor, "could you help us a little? We're lost."

"Sure you are," said the rider. "That's 'cuz you ain't got no business out here."

"We're just passing through," said Wifey. "We just can't find this road on our map. Some signs with numbers would help."

"And that ain't none of *my* business, or yours. Exactly where you are ain't none of your business."

I looked around to see if we were still sitting by a church—and we were.

"Just a number by the side of the road—something like what is on the maps..." Wifey offered. Her Long Island accent resonated.

"You come out here from the city and you want to change everything. Why cain't you jist leave things alone? We don't have no road signs because we don't want no road signs." (And I could understand that. The county's roads set the place apart from other places. They caused terror, disorientation, and consequently prayer. Why change that?)

"But why don't you want road signs?" Wifey persisted. It was my turn. I started kicking Wifey to shut her up. My earworm was getting loud.

"'Cuz they clutter up the landscape—destroy the beauty, and attract city folks. Cain't you just appreciate the beauty and go home?" This was ironic, I thought, because we had seen—and heeded—ten thousand "No Hunting or Trespassing" signs protecting property littered with wrecked cars and rusted household appliances. Eyesores, I say. But I did not comment on that.

"We can appreciate the beauty, but we can't go home because we don't know where we are," I offered, innocently, quietly.

"And whose fault is that? We's jist out here mindin' our own business, like you ought to be doin', and you bounce in here all lost. We may be dumb, and we may be inbred, but we ain't lost!"

Well, I could tell he had seen *Deliverance*, too, or inspired it. We had never said anything about anybody being dumb or about anybody's gene pool being shallow, and we did not appreciate being credited with such thoughts. We didn't comment, though, because I think Wifey was beginning to hear the banjo music, too. She started the engine.

"Nice talking to you," said Wifey, gunning the motor. "We're outa here."

Then the fellows waved their arms, stopped us, got together on giving us some directions—off the edge of the earth, into a box canyon, through a river, up a cliff, over a mile or two of busted rock—just exactly where Wifey wanted to go. They could have been *mis*directions—or just plain meanness—for someone not interested in extreme riding. Wifey just gunned the engine again and plummeted off into the wilderness, wildly happy.

"Thank you," I yelled back as we yanked away. I was happier at that moment, too. Wifey sped up and we put miles of uncharted road between us and them.

For the first time, though, I watched the ridges and treelines for riflemen and "good ol' boys" rather than bears, bobcats, and "beasties." For the first time in six years, we had been told that we were not wanted. (You can't win 'em all.) I wondered if this man's view was widely held, or if, after seeing bears, deer, wild turkeys, emus, bobcats, skunks, coons, possums, rattlesnakes, armadillos, goats, llamas, cattle, horses, elk, copperheads, and wild pigs, we had just seen our first real jackass. For the first time in a long time, I was angry.

***

I got over it. I understand being misunderstood. My accustomed earworm is back now, and I like it better: "How Great Thou Art." That's what I think about most of the time when I view the vistas from high up—from the main numbered highway—where I belong. But, you know, every time I look at that ATV, I hear a banjo: Ringa-ding *ding* ding!—and a guitar answers from down in the woods. A reminder.

THE JAWS OF LIFE

Wifey and her shopping buddies Lacy and Rita had just pulled into the driveway. It was late, and darkness was taking over the high country, and the wind was whipping up. I was at the window, waiting, worrying. Silly of me. What could possibly go wrong with a simple shopping excursion, right?

But I could tell right away that something *had* gone wrong. Wifey hit the ground running toward the house, and Rita jumped out of our little truck, then leaned back in, working on something.

I headed Wifey off by opening the front door. "Get out here," she yelled. "We've got to have some help." She turned back.

I dug around clumsily for some matching disposable shoes in the pile by the door—a pair about evenly worn or paint-splotched—as I pulled on a light jacket. Whatever was wrong out there now involved me. I knew it was going to be one of those weird female developments that I never seemed to get the hang of.

"A mere man, with 'original equipment,' is not set up to understand women," the voice of my advisor Double-Dog Darrell nagged as I struggled with the shoes, the jacket, the door, and the steps. "Ask no questions, Pilgrim. Just breathe." I had asked about woman stuff during one of our consultations, and that's all he had for me. I was unprepared and utterly clueless as I dashed out to the truck.

I saw immediately what had happened. I saw, but I did not necessarily believe or understand. One of the shoppers was trapped.

***

The women had not been simply shopping. They had been

"thrift shopping"—a genre of *Extreme Shopping.* It was a clubby thing: an amusement, a challenge and a game. They would run a route among several second-hand stores—in two or three counties, sometimes in two states—and "salvage" items that had lost the interest of other owners. Today it had been Wifey's turn to drive. Rita Roller, in particular, had an uncanny knack for taking irrelated pieces of discarded miscellany and assembling something decorative or useful.

The stores had cute, sometimes rhyming titles like Used and Abused, Share and Repair, Twice Is Nice, or Then and Again, or Scratches and Dings and Lovely Things; OR Two Timers, or Once More With Feeling, or Yours, Mine, and Yours Again. I had been dragged everywhere on such treasure hunts in Wifey's valiant quest to stuff every cubic inch of our spare room.

Of course, there was an element of charity in all of it. People (including all of the "girls" and me) had donated the items for sale at the stores, and the money would ultimately go to worthy causes. That was good. And they were good places to pick up painting togs, work pants, rags, even items of household hardware, used tools, remnants of building supplies, etc. Re-cycling, for Heaven's Sake! But the girls were hooked on the stuff, and the whole process had become a competition: Who could come up with the most outrageous bargain? With no regard for, Who knows when to quit? They were addicted—all of them.

Lacy, as I immediately perceived, was crammed into the back seat of our little truck, and there did not seem to be much hope of extricating her. She had missed the last two stops of the tour because she could not get out of the vehicle: she was jammed in there and buried by then. Still there had been further purchases of even more items, and a lot of wedging and tamping had gone on. Now, there were just two horribly still eyes peering out from the compressed plug of second-hand treasures that formed an absolute bale in the back seat.

No, none of the stuff could have gone outside in the box of the truck. It had been raining, and the fiberglass lid, which normally protected the box from the weather, lay in the grass by the garage. (We had removed the heavy cover so that the new ATV would fit into the box to be hauled close to wherever Wifey needed to ride.) It was an extended-cab truck, so there was just a small, cramped back seat. Earlier in the day, Lacy had foolishly bragged about her flexibility (indeed, Lacy was an athlete, very active, always on the move), and so she had ended up being the one stuffed into that back seat. Now it seemed hopeless.

Lacy's breathing was labored and shallow, and her eyes were crossed and dilated, but Wifey thought she could save her without CPR if we could just somehow get hold of something and jerk her out of there. (Wifey used some fancy nursing terminology and waved a tiny flashlight at the eyes.)

"We've got to get her out of there, and soon," said Wifey with great concern. "We don't want any of her special sensors damaged. She can detect a thrift shop at a distance of seven miles—more if the wind's right."

This was going to be like digging out trapped miners, or getting Baby Jessica out of the well, or "taking" a baby with instruments. I could imagine a sound like a huge cork popping loose. I thought about a winch or a "come-along." We had to help Lacy, and free her, no matter what—and very soon.

I knew that I was at a critical moment—not just for Lacy, but also for me. If I chose this instant to ask why or how, I would be doomed. "Ask no questions," Double-Dog Darrell's words echoed, "just breathe." I spoke not a word, but moved in for a closer look .

Right under Lacy's chin was a bread machine, and wedged up against her left cheek was some sort of stuffed animal. (I think we had donated it a year before.) She had a blender up against her right cheek, and some of Rita's latest curtains were on top of Lacy's head. (Rita had no windows in her apartment. Don't ask.) A trembling hand emerged from a pile of video tapes and shoe trees on the driver's side. The hand was a peculiar blue, but it showed she was fighting back—alive in there somewhere. Somehow, there were lamp shades and fruit jars, paintings, wooden salad forks and spoons, roosters for Wifey's collection, pumpkins for Lacy's, beads and colored glass for Rita's. Somewhere down deep, a can of whipped cream was spraying. Lacy's feet were immobilized by rocks from a creek bed in Missouri and driftwood from Bull Shoals Lake. There was a bird cage, too, and sphagnum moss—and some potting soil. There was some loose yarn right by Lacy's nose, part of a butter dish, a plastic yard ornament, a basket or two, and some plastic flowers—that I could see. It looked to me like a job for "The Jaws of Life," but I spoke not.

Then I heard a pathetic, tiny voice. I looked at the eyes, and one of them blinked, and then I heard, very distinctly, "Help." Calm, quiet, irresistible. "Help me."

My heart skipped a beat. I could very well be a hero here, if I played my cards right. I could get the Medal of Freedom or something for heroism above and beyond the call of...never mind. I would save the day.

I comforted her with the only words I could think of. "Ask no questions, Pilgrim. Just breathe."

I was reaching for the blue hand when Wifey stopped me. "We can't just yank her out. We have to unpack her. You'll ruin our merchandise."

"Yes, Dear."

I was perplexed. I looked at the pressurized melange, the pitiful eyes, and the problem. It was complicated, dicey, maybe a little dangerous. Light was fading, too. I had to think of something.

Then I spotted a detail, and a stratagem instantly exploded in my fevered mind. "How about this?" I said, and I began pulling on the piece of yarn by Lacy's nose. I reasoned that if it was a long enough piece of yarn and I pulled on it for a while, I might loosen the whole log jam—or at least prevent further strangulation.

"That's my Afghan!" screamed Wifey. "Leave that alone!"

"Yes, Dear." I pulled my hand back just in time to save it.

It was one of those moments when a man wants to step back and give his wife that well-rehearsed "what the hell are you thinking?" look, but there was no time.

I could have pulled a bushel of yarn out of that mess and freed Lacy quickly. I was sure. Failure. It was time for Plan C or D or whatever. Lacy's nails and lips were blue, and she was frighteningly still. I found an elbow and nudged it a bit, but it did not move.

I tried the bread machine, but Lacy's screams stopped that. Pretty good scream, too, with so little air. I was looking for the keystone. Often there is one particular component in a wall like this, and if you remove it, the whole thing crumbles. I grabbed hold of a stainless steel knob and gave it a twist. No scream, but no action, either. It was part of some kitchen utensil or container, I was sure. I wiggled it left, then right. Nothing but moans. I tried rotating the knob. No progress.

Then I thought about Wifey's foreign-made American car. It was full of strange latches and hitches, catches and glitches, all left-handed and metric. I had encountered all of them. I pushed in, gave the knob a small twist, and then pulled back. Bayonet mount! Who knew? It came out, and Lacy gave forth a great sigh. Triumphantly, I threw the thing out into the driveway without looking at it. Lacy was moving.

Rita had gone into the house and now emerged with a clothes basket, and we all began freeing the tightly-packed items and tossing them into the basket. Wifey gently placed some of the goods in the truck box, temporarily, of course. Gradually, Lacy was reborn: we got hold of her and eased her out of the back seat, brushed her off, and stood her on her feet and leaned her against the truck, then wiped the whipped cream off her shoes. The color came back into her face slowly, and eventually her blue hand turned pinkish. Wifey's nursing instincts took over then, and I stepped back.

"Lacy!" said, Wifey. "Look at me!"

Lacy was groggy, but she slowly focused.

"Now, Lacy, concentrate," said Wifey. "Exactly where is the nearest thrift shop?"

Instantly, Lacy pointed toward the village and said, "Angel Works, Jasper. Seven miles, plus one hundred yards."

There was a great sigh of relief all around. The "Unit" had survived. She was good to go.

***

I later learned that the stainless steel knob had something to do with part of a federal-case mixer Wifey was pulling together a piece at a time. And somewhere in the knotted gallimaufry of that back seat there was the top to a frosted glass butter dish. The top only, mind you. The bottom? Well that was declared the object of the next quest. All three of them were certain that it was out there somewhere. One of them had actually seen it. But where? Where?

I'm told that Lacy has dibs on the front seat.

Me? I'm not in on it. I ask no questions. I just breathe. These matters make sense to womankind, whether I understand or not. I'm retired, and I'm going for bliss all the way.

CLAWING TOGETHER SOME CHRISTMAS

Children's stories make it clear that Christmas will come—whether or not there is snow for Santa's reindeer and sleigh, a chimney for him to come down, or enough prosperity for milk and cookies. It will come, no matter who is being a Grinch or a Scrooge, no matter who is at war or at peace, no matter how intense the traffic of current events. And it will come despite denial, old age, or politics. Or weather. We sell all of that pretty hard. Christmas is bigger than those things.

In later life, after children and even grandchildren (or not), we find that Christmas will indeed come, relentlessly, no matter how many times we have seen it, and no matter what we have done to prevent it or circumvent it, or re-invent it. It comes, with song and poem, with story and imagery, with joy and pain, and memories, no matter what. And its meaning broadens and deepens as it runs over us and flattens us.

On our remote mountain top, Christmas always arrived, whether or not I dragged down the nearly forgotten boxes from the rafters of the garage—or strung up the touchy sometimes lights for the phony tree inside and the real ones outside—or escaped Wifey to wander hopelessly at Wal-Mart seeking the perfect, pacifying gift to get her through it and me off the hook. (She ran similar patterns, in all fairness.) Christmas came, all right, and both of us would be looking for a way out—especially a way out of Christmas Eve.

The life we had chosen looked a lot like self-imposed exile at Christmas. On our ridge, miles from town and two weeks further into winter, there could be a bleakness about it: the colors of autumn gone, a gray cast to the woods, a lonesome wind at night, some cold, probably no snow (later, usually), and a distinct lull in the tourist/

resort activity and atmosphere. For us that meant a lot of planned travel off mountain to vacation spots or relatives' homes, if possible. Otherwise, Christmas would be one-on-one, on a lonely mountain.

We had chosen—and sacrificed. When you are alone by choice, you have no right to self-pity—and it would be an insult, when you stop to think about it. If you pity yourself for being alone with yourself, you do have a problem. Wifey and I were okay, most of the time: alone together. Like so many of our neighbors, we had retreated selfishly from cities and complications, and, alas, families and friends, to experience economy, privacy, tranquility, and distinct seasons in our "golden" years. And we got it all, and it was wonderful most of the year, but Christmas could be difficult. Hey, Christmas *was* difficult. People like us were reminded of all we had left behind.

***

One year Wifey and I had been successful in the pre-Christmas phase of things. We had punched up our wardrobes and done a cruise in the Bermuda Triangle (tempting Fate)—our gifts to each other—and after that we had done a little Branson. After the cruise it would be unnecessary to eat again until Spring, and after Silver Dollar City and Shoji Tabuchi, Dino, and three or four other Branson musical shows, it would be unnecessary to light up any trees or spread around any tinsel or do anything glitzy or festive anytime soon, thank you. We had been there, done that, amen. Overkill, in fact. We had "gotten that out of the way." (As if you could really do that.) We strung up a mess of lights and called it a day. In January we would escape some winter and go see the relatives and old friends. Lots of us "rim folk" did something like that. It was all set.

***

And then the lights went out—literally. One of our patented ice storms nailed us at just exactly the most inconvenient moment.

All previous thinking and planning became irrelevant as the whole county stopped—after a short skid—and froze.

It is a phenomenon familiar to locals. Just about at the Missouri/Arkansas line, there is a target—one of God's zany little playgrounds—and quite often it gets bombed with goodly inches of pesky, damaging, slippery, clear blue ice. It often blind-sides us because we don't believe the weathermen anymore—not really. The electrical power goes off, the roads shut down, the whole world becomes so beautiful it weakens your knees, and most traffic just stops—or skids off the mountains.

Rick Roller and his wife Rita had just made it up the hill—having stayed in the town an instant too long. They split their time between where Rick wanted to be (romping through the woods on an ATV) and where Rita wanted to be. It was Rita's turn now: home with the family for Christmas. They dropped by our outpost (just for a moment, mind you) to say Goodbye and Merry Christmas, then they were to zoom off on their way South, going home to kids and grandkids, and Christmas trees and lights, and…never mind. They never left our driveway. We got to talking about the wonderful summer and fall of wild ATV activity, swimming, exploration, freedom, and fun, and time passed. The storm hit fast and slightly ahead of schedule. We now had guests, that was all. Their Christmas with the family would have to wait.

Double-Dog Darrell, we discovered later, had succeeded in finding a lady on the Internet and conning her into a visit. Down in his lair amid the boulders at the mouth of the cave a mile or so down off the other side of Scenic Byway Seven, he and the lady were almost immobilized by the ice. Cozy, but hardly festive. Getting out of there was not something for an ordinary car, and you wouldn't do that to a horse, not even an experienced horse like Darrell's. They were all trapped: man, woman, horse, wolves, all. Well, almost trapped.

Old Zeke, a man who always seemed to have the inside story on everything even though he lived in almost total isolation, had made it out to the highway from his hermitage, way out and beyond—off the end of the tether and then some, but he had been unable to hitch a ride anywhere because of the lack of traffic. (He never did tell us where he proposed to go.) He was stuck out there along the road, turning into an icicle, when our mob found him.

Old Rathbone, I regret to say, had managed to get himself into our area, too—just in time for the ice. He had reached safety just as the lights went out. Luckily, he had stumbled onto our "too-close" neighbor's place rather than ours, but there he was: in my space, in my face, and full of attitude. I certainly did not need any more of his condescension. But we were on a collision course, and we could not navigate. I found Old Rathbone stumbling around in the narrow strip of woods just at the end of our clothesline, and I reeled him in.

And we already had Old Mr. Hooper at our place. His idea was that you started the next year's garden ten minutes after Christmas, and that moment came on Christmas Eve, and he was our garden mentor. Therefore, what with food considerations and all, it was just natural that he be with us. We needed him, too. It was always Christmas when Mr. Hooper was around. He had outlived all other potential Christmas companions anyway, had left a lot behind. He was our house guest when things got, well, slippery. But he was safe and we were happy.

Just down the highway from us about a mile, a potential tragedy was unfolding. A pair of our neighbors (about our vintage but more into family ties) had prepared a knock-down-drag-out celebration of everything scrumptious for a batch of relatives who were coming in from all over. In a flurry of phone calls, however, every one of the relatives had cancelled, citing Highway Patrol warnings, TV bulletins, anecdotal information, and Weather Channel reports. Ice.

"I don't know what I'm going to do," Jolene told Wifey on the phone. "I've got a twenty-pound turkey about roasted, and I've got a fifteen-pound ham ready—and all the trimmings! And nobody's coming!"

"I'm so sorry," said Wifey, carefully. This was going to be delicate.

"And it was my last one, too. Next year my daughters are doing the dinner—on Christmas Day, in Russellville. After that, my son's place in Springdale. Then, who knows? But what can I do? Darn."

"Darn," repeated Wifey, gesturing wildly for me to get on the other phone.

"Such a problem. You just never know about these ice storms," Jolene said.

"Let me think," said Wifey. And Wifey, who did not need to think at all, patiently held the phone and went into deep, deep thought. "Hmmm...no telling how long we'll be trapped here."

I had an idea, of course. I am fast at these things. All of us in our family were quick with ideas—and helpful, too. Always. "How about we all come over and pig out!" I wanted to suggest, but I knew I would be kicked half to death by Wifey—over the phone! So I did not speak.

"I suppose I could just freeze the stuff," muttered Jolene.

"Don't freeze the stuff!" I wanted to scream, but didn't. I nearly strangled restraining myself.

"Oh, you have electricity?" asked Wifey. Incisive, I thought.

"Oh, no we don't. I can't freeze it. Darn."

"Darn," confirmed Wifey.

Wifey kept her composure. We had already declined an earlier invitation to Jolene's event, not wanting to be in the way of family traditions. But now the family was out of it. Wifey struggled, but she came up with a suitably neutral position. "If the power should come on and you decide to freeze the turkey, you risk drying it out. But I could check my cook books..."

"Don't check your cook books!" I almost whined into the phone. Almost.

"*I know,*" said Jolene at last, "*why don't you just come on over here? We'll just claw together a little Christmas the best way we can! And bring your friends. It'll be like an extended family.*"

"Well, I suppose I could bring some fresh-baked bread, a few pickles... I guess we could—if we can get there...what the heck, let's do it!" said Wifey. (It was touch and go there for a while.)

"You get here, and we'll have a party," said Jolene. "And find anybody else that you can!" Jolene felt better already, and I did too. Christmas was happening!

Wifey agreed, quietly, telling Jolene that it was a great idea. Then she put down the phone, leaped in the air, and screamed, "Yes!" It was a gig. She told us the good news, word for word, and she led us all in a little touchdown dance, even Old Hooper.

Always, but *always*, we were ready for a pig-out. On Christmas Eve, we were game for anything. But this was spectacular. We would bring Old Hooper, Rick and Rita, maybe even the cat. It was all good. There would be quite a mob! Oh, and we had Old Rathbone chained in the cellar. (Not really. Wishful thinking on my part.) Maybe there were others out there in the ice.

Hey, Deck the Halls, right?

Jolene and Jake had gas heat and a gas stove for all the cooking, but tons of left-overs would be a problem—without us, all of us, and then some. No, we would be forced to go over there and do our damndest to prevent waste. (Wifey and I have become very civic minded and socially conscious in our old age.)

"As I see it," said Rathbone, our he-had-no-idea-how-temporary houseguest, "we have an obligation here. If we don't eat that food, someone might send it to Iraq." And I, for one, agreed with Rathbone, for a change.

The whole ridge went into action. Wifey triggered an immediate phone fan-out; Rick Roller and Wifey then ventured forth on ATVs to collect stranded stragglers; Jake, our host, put some chains on his truck and went searching the neighborhood— with Old Rathbone riding shotgun; Rita Roller scampered around like Martha Stewart and made extra decorations and party favors out of what seemed like thin air; and (long story made short) the indigenous mountain top personnel were rounded up, thawed out, and delivered to the feast site.

I, of course, assumed a supervisory role. (Diet Coke, and a little rum, with icicles right off the house! And the telephone. I was good in there. I insist. I even got out some fudge from our freezer. I was not idle. Someone has to handle the logistical work. Shut up.)

***

A beautiful, unfinished house was sitting right on top of the party—literally. Jolene and Jake had been living in a large basement apartment for a few years, making plans and gathering materials, etc. Jake was building the house himself, lots of it with his own hands, and it was finally going well. It was "weathered in," and ready for plumbing and heating and finishing. Under the house, in the basement apartment, the feast awaited us. We carefully edged our way around back to the magic door, genuinely awed by Jake's work, and happy for Jolene. Her new house was happening!

Felix Dalby, Sculptor, was already at the party when our contingent arrived. The hostess had found him, all divorced and everything, and invited him to the bash. He had dominated last fall's County Fair with his bullet-riddled Jeep "sculpture," and so he was an entity, but it was his pathetic demeanor that had attracted our hostess. He needed rescuing. It was I, of course, who arranged his transportation. I contacted Moose Vandergrift (who protects me), and he managed with his Hummer to pick up Felix at some slippery rendezvous down in the woods. Both were fashionably clad in camouflage. Their arrival had been spectacular, Jolene told us.

I never did learn whether Justin Kase, local poet, was part of the original guest list or a pick-up, fill-in, substitute, pinch-hitter type-of-thing, but he was there with his notebook ready to immortalize the whole event, probably in iambic pentameter or something equally classic. Jolene seemed to know him well. She had an interest in poetry, too.

Wifey and Rick Roller picked up Double-Dog Darrell and his Internet lady (both in fur and leather outfits) and somehow got them up the icy hill on ATVs, and another fellow vaguely familiar to me materialized somehow, on foot, I believe. (He wore pressed jeans. That always bothered me. We had once moved a piano together—for Double-Dog Darrell. Somewhere, this guy had a

Mercedes.) Someone told me later that there was an actual by-God atheist at the party, and a pair of gay women. I don't know how they got there, and I couldn't tell which was which by looking at them. I don't think any of them hurt anything. Ordinarily, nobody cares about politics when there's food, anyway.

There was egg nog, and there was real brown-bottle refreshment, and there were clear substances native to the area (and probably dangerous), and from Russia and Mexico, and the deliberations began. I drifted among conversations.

Some of us had outgrown Christmas, but not the need for it. Old Rathbone tore into me about the commercialization of the holidays. It was apparently all my fault. While I was stiff-arming him, I learned that the old coot was two years younger than I was! For many months, I had been getting all kinds of fatherly advice from some kid who was barely eligible for his Social Security check! Go figure. I dismissed him completely after that.

Old Zeke Davidshofer, in full Dogpatch regalia despite the short notice, had read a popular book, and now he was convinced that Christ was a married man—the inside story, at last—and a father to boot. So, I joked that Jesus probably married Mary Magdalene, and Old Zeke was impressed with my incisive thinking, my rebellious sacrilege. (I failed to mention that I had read the same book.) Zeke went on to say that he had always suspected that one of our closest neighbors was a descendant of that couple. (He was able to claim a history of deep thought even about ideas brand new to him.)

Rick Roller claimed he could take us to a rock formation that looked like the Manger Itself. I mentioned that I had seen shepherds from the back of Wifey's ATV while careening down a mountain, and that I shot pool with the wise men. Nobody was amused, so I didn't even laugh myself. Mr. Hooper had a story about a Depression Era Christmas squirrel fry in Southern Illinois. Rita Roller found candles and mirrors and lit the whole place up like...well, you know.

Point is, the conversation—and just about everything else at the party—became rather Christmassy. We agreed that no

Christmas decorations had ever been as beautiful as all that ice. Memories of other ice in other years, other parties in other times and marriages and places, and other people in other thrown-together, fun and desperate situations (including war) livened the babble. Nobody admitted to any loneliness or regret.

Justin Kase, with the imagined icy wind in his face, scarf flowing, recited from his latest unfinished poem:

> It was Christmas, all right, up and down Highway Seven,
> And the kiddies were there: every Kyle, Bob and Kevin—
> All the Suzy's and Sally's and other young cuties—
> The Dolly's and Daisy's and Ruby's and Judy's.
> And up on the ridge where it's all snow and ice,
> We had a big party, and life was just nice.
> There was Rathbone, ensconced with his nose in the air,
> And Hooper was there in the old rocking chair;
> We had Rita and Rick and Old Zeke, don't forget—
> And Double-Dog's gal from the Internet…

The Great Poet made no excuses, took no prisoners. Was it poetry? I don't know. It was Christmas. Whadeya gonna do? He was being the classic New England Poet in winter. I just know there was a moaning wind.

Even Moose Vandergrift had an amusing comment or two, but nobody understood much, including me. I was too awed by the sight of Moose indoors, in a tight space, with people. Moose, inside a house; Moose, sitting down; Moose, with a cup of egg nog; Moose, near cooked food. Moose, and Christmas. It was like having a…well, a moose, in the breakfast nook. We laughed at his garbled comments. He did say, "Ho ho ho," and everybody picked up on that.

Our host was playing "The First Noel" on a banjo. (You don't hear that a lot.) Wifey and Rita Roller helped the hostess in the kitchen, and the Internet lady pitched in, too—and of course, Double-Dog Darrell carved. (I hated to see him with that big knife, but he was medicated, and it worked out.) I guess those other ladies were probably the lesbians. (Nobody ever tells me anything critical in time.) And, just as we were about to fill up our plates, Cowboy Jess, in formal cowboy attire, made the scene with bottles of domestic (Big Creek Valley) wine: home-made and utterly shattering. His hat barely fit into the room, and there was snow on it.

The big underground room was warm and full; Rita's candles were everywhere; the aromas and scents of all that food embraced us and made us ravenously hungry (mint and cinnamon, sage and nutmeg, and peanut butter); all worries and cares were put on hold for the duration; and the host raised his fork and conducted as we sang "Silent Night" like a choir—all of us, including the alleged atheist. Then someone said grace, and we dug in. Like a large, unruly family.

***

We did have one little reversal—or irony—later on at the party. Upstairs, the main house was "lumbering" toward completion—weathered in (sealed off from the outside)—slowly turning into a dwelling. And to get up there from the basement party scene for a guided tour without going outside, we all went up the chimney, with flashlights! (Well, up the "well" where the chimney would soon be built.) After Big Valley wine, too! Even Old Mr. Hooper! Up a ladder! (Moose shoved.) The huge void was spooky and shadowy and cold—and full of potential: raw lumber now, but certainly a party site for the future. Cavernous and cold, but no longer empty. Our host, who knew each board personally, told his tale, from inspiration to realized fact—by flashlight, with frosty breath. And then, out of the blue, we all sang "Bless This House." And I think we sort of breathed life into the building right there. Everybody felt something. Go figure.

We had clawed together a pretty good little Christmas after all, for older folks.

THE GRAVITY OF THE SITUATION

There is something that does not want us at the top—in any respect: something that wants us down. It doesn't want us living on top of mountains, and it doesn't want us at the top of our game, in the best of health, at peace, terribly content, or exorbitantly happy. Or attractive. Or young!

Gravity.

Who was ready? Who knew? Who cared? Certainly not I. Not Wifey. We had scoped out the whole United States, after all, and come up with a retirement home clinging precariously to a cliff! In a place called Newton County. (Who knew it would be about THAT Newton—the *gravity* Newton?) I was thinking "fig" all the way. Unfair, I say.

I had noticed as it exerted its influence on others around me. Hair was slipping over the sides of the heads of those old guys in the audiences at Branson. Socks, I had noticed, were slipping down old stringy legs, pants were hanging low on disappearing hips, chests were slipping down and becoming bellies. Breasts were sagging. And that was just the men! Poor devils.

I was amused, at first. It was a shame what was happening to those guys, a pity and a tragedy. I was glad it was their problem and not mine.

But time passed, and my life went into one of those downward spirals you hear about. I gained weight, but then I valiantly lost weight in a spectacular diet/exercise sequence. The weight loss caused all the stuffing to go out of one of my chins, and my neck developed this withered drape of skin that hung there like a shroud, mocking me. A revolting development! It jiggled and swung back and forth when I tried to shave. In a video tape of myself, I saw that light would actually pass through the thing! It was a disappointing, humiliating, flaccid manifestation: a betrayal!—and I decided that I hated it. Even the mirror seemed embarrassed for me. I didn't discuss it with Wifey. I prayed for some sort of remission..

Then, one of our feral cats (a hussy for sure) presented us with a litter of kittens: made sure that we knew about them and shared the ownership. So they were suddenly around—cute and tiny and vulnerable, and just there. I knew that, and I tried to be sympathetic and supportive, though uninvolved. But in a moment of weakness one afternoon, I fell asleep on the couch, and Wifey—ever the tender-hearted soul—placed one of those new kittens on what was left of my chest. I awoke to find the critter trying to nurse on a little brown mole it had discovered—poised there on a fold in that disgusting deflated chin of mine!

Now, I like to help out where I can. I am a responsible person and an AARP member, and I like to think I pitch in. But how much can you ask of a dignified man? Imagine how I struggled with the situation—how I agonized! Most men never face such poignant moments. (I have asked around. Quietly.) Should I just lie there and take it, risking setting a bad precedent, or should I take gentle corrective measures? Or should I fling the cat through the wall? A momentary enigma.

I jumped up and streaked to the mirror, forfeiting the couch to the kitten. I had taken to spending very little time around mirrors, but this occasion had me curious. I had to bite the bullet and take look at myself, seriously, and critically.

The site of the suckling attack was a little red, but not seriously injured. I could understand the kitten's mistake, now that I looked closely. Then I took a good look at the rest of my face. The corners of my mouth turned downward now, my eyelids drooped a bit, some jowls had begun to develop, my nose seemed larger than ever, there was a pervasive sag about things in general. Gravity. I had never considered myself as sad as I appeared in that mirror, but all was even now. I was what I was. My face had caught up with my age. I couldn't bear to look at my body. Thank God the mirror cut me off at the waist.

***

Who knew that gravity was going to become *the* significant enemy of my Golden Years? And who knew how embarrassing gravity could be?

It became painfully obvious, the more I thought about it. The rules were clear enough. *We could keep our house and its magnificent view for only so long. All too soon one of us would not be able to "cut it" on the mountain. One of us would come down with "bad knees" or a "bad back" or "bad ankles" or a "bum ticker"—or something else bad or bum—and the other would not be physically capable of hanging on for both. We would be torn loose by this cruel gravity thing and have to live in town, down hill, forced into merely remembering our dream. We were just hanging on by the fingernails.*

Oh, it was always there. You don't just come down with gravity one day. I had been in denial, but now I started adding things up, and it turned out that I knew a little about gravity. There had been moments.

I remembered the day I was walking out to work on the cabin out back, and my two-liter bottle of Diet Coke got away from me and headed off down mountain. Ever the competitor, I ran it down after about sixty feet—got my foot in front of it and stopped it cold—just as it exploded and sprayed its blessed juices up my nose, down my neck, into my face, my glasses, my overalls. (I wish I had control of Wifey's video tape of that!)

"Why are you sucking on your bib overalls?" she asked sweetly when she caught up to me.

"Diet Coke is expensive," I told her, "and I hate to waste it." It was all I could salvage. What can I say? I am a frugal man. It seemed like a good idea at the time.

Ever go cart-wheeling with a wheelbarrow? Same type of thing, really. I skied the slope out back on an aluminum ladder once, too.

And a few acorns or black walnuts can make you absolutely fly—with a little help from gravity. Yeah, I knew a little.

Wifey had been amused when my cargo dolly, on several occasions, had arbitrarily broken loose and led me on a merry chase down the back slope. I was never able to gain on it, and was always forced to drag it up out of the heavy brush inside the debris line at the bottom of our yard where it had stopped. Fifty vertical feet down.

Oh, yes, a debris line! It was festive at times. (At least that's the word I used on Wifey.) At the lower edge of our "manicured" area out back, there developed a colorful furrow of sorts made up of blue plastic Wal-Mart bags, white bags from Bob's Market, aluminum foil, pie tins, lawn furniture, hanging baskets, Styrofoam fast food and drink containers and disposable diapers from Highway Seven tourists, underwear and socks from our clothesline, insulation, dead animals, trash we had tried and failed to burn. Anything light or round or just smooth. All of it would dive down there and hang up in the briars, awaiting re-capture. In the wind, it was chaotic! But pretty! Festive. I insist. A good thing.

"If you have any Martha Stewart in you at all, you will go down there and put together a wreath," I told Wifey.

"Wifey doesn't do Martha Stewart," she said.

Wifey doesn't do gravity, either. She has some sort of nurse syndrome. One day I got out of my recliner and told Wifey I was going to put on some boots and go out back and do a little trimming. When I emerged from the bedroom all suited up, she handed me a sack of trash and a pail of compostable material (for out back), then she draped some clean clothes over my shoulder (for the downstairs bedroom). Under my right arm she tucked a pillow case full of dirty clothes (for the laundry room, downstairs). She put her straw hat on my head (to be taken downstairs), and under my left arm she placed a four-foot level—a tool I had been using (which belonged in the garage). At the head of the stairs, she hooked a Wal-Mart bag full of Diet Coke cans to my left pinky (for re-cycling), and put a screwdriver in my mouth (to be returned to the garage also). She jammed the bib of my overalls with carpenter's pencils and an ATV manual.

"Careful on those steps," she told me. "I don't want to have to hunt up another Sherpa."

I told her, "Mhgrph lmbchk yrngols cnwql!" which means, "Yes Dear," I promise. I later learned to talk well with a screwdriver in my mouth.

***

Gravity is subtle and sneaky, and sometimes it operates in disguise. We were certain that The Compound had been infiltrated and sabotaged by a bear on one occasion. The trash barrels disappeared, and I found them out in the woods several yards from where they belonged. Certainly it would take a large animal to move those steel barrels, right? But no: once they were tipped over by the coons, gravity did the rest, probably. I needed a bear, however, to help put the barrels back.

One of Wifey's girlfriends, Annie, was just home from shopping, even though it was late and dark and spooky on her mountain. Like us, Annie tried not to drive the mountain roads in the dark—tried to get all the business done in daylight. Things jump out in front of your car in the mountains at night, and the curves are sharp. And you don't know what's waiting for you in your yard.

Annie stopped the car close to the house and unloaded a box of groceries and a heavy watermelon from the trunk of her sedan and set them aside, then put the car away in the garage several yards away. When she returned to pick up the groceries, the melon was gone. The box of groceries was still there. She searched and wondered and scratched her head, and then finally gave up. Annie solved the mystery of what happened to her melon the next Spring when she found several volunteer watermelon vines merrily growing in a ditch, many yards away from the house—downhill!—at the lower edge of her property. Melons are round. Gravity had struck again.

When I crawled to the house one icy winter day, bleeding and bruised, my clothes tattered and shredded, Wifey was certain I had been mugged. Truth was, I had just made a mistake and skidded about eighty feet down the back acreage—on three-inch ice. Just one small error.

I often found tools, baskets, and buckets down in the woods— after a little lapse here or there. A railroad tie I was using for a retaining wall got away from me one morning, and it's still down there somewhere. After it ran over me, I didn't chase it anymore, or care about it. Sometimes, while retrieving this or that, I found items Wifey had been wondering about: hanging baskets, potted plants, laundry items.

Wifey and I learned to make the best of it, and to rationalize. "All right, we're clinging to a cliff here. But we can see forty miles! It's beautiful...No, we don't play much croquet here...Everybody should set their emergency brake anyway! The brush down there stopped your car, ma'am, and we'll find it...Hey, downhill, uphill, downhill—it's good exercise. Where's the downside? Never mind...Okay, ice and steepness don't go well together, but the dog will come home, eventually. Lassie came home. Sometimes if you just set your foot on their little tails...Yes, it's slippery, but we live in a crystal chandelier here! It's beautiful...Hey, you don't want to fall out of ANY hammock. Quit complaining...We will invent an outrigger for the lawnmower! Besides, when the mower gets three wheels off the ground at once, it shuts off! No problemo...Kid? What kid? I didn't know you had a kid with you. We'll just go find him. I'm guessing downhill...We don't have to pick the peaches: we just get a fielder's glove and set up downhill from the tree. We don't mind chasing our crops. The pumpkins grow up and leave home. No problemo! Sorry, Timmy, I haven't seen your ball. Round, wasn't it? Not good. Maybe we could put an ad in *The Valley Times*...Sure, it's more of a cliff than a yard, but, hey, we're part of the sky here—people look up to us! It's beautiful...Careful, black walnuts underfoot! Sorry about that."

It was fun visiting us, back when people visited us.

So far, we've run into only one dependable solution to the

gravity problem: the valley. The town's down there. When we're through up on top, we'll go down there, and when it's not cloudy, we'll look back up to the mountain—past Scenic Point—and we'll remember.

***

Down in the village there's a man who has a wonderful garden. I noted his success, and one day I visited his garden, and I had to ask him, "Jerry, where did you get this beautiful soil?"

"Washed down from your place," he said. I believed him then, and I believe him now.

Art by Scott Baldassari.

*H*anging *On for Dear Life* available in Jasper, AR from the author, personally autographed at(gwbkgn@jasper.yourne t.com) or 870-446-2408, at the Newton County Chamber of Commerce, Emma's Museum of Junk, Scenic Point, and other area gift shops. Also by Gary Weibye: *Teetering on the Brink* and *The Demons of Daylight* online at www.booksurge.com *or* 866-308-6235. *Sanity by Sunrise, a night of post-teaching stress syndrome* available at xlibris.com *or* 888-795-4274 x. 276.

1183113

Made in the USA